A GaWaNi Pony Boy Book

OF WOMEN AND HORSES

Essays by Various Horsewomen

Illustrated by Various Artists — Photographs by Gabrielle Boiselle

BOWTIE
PRESS

A Division of Fancy Publications
Irvine, California

Commentary by GaWaNi Pony Boy, author of

Horse, Follow Closely

Ruth Berman, editor-in-chief
Nick Clemente, special consultant
Amy Fox, editor
Book design © 2000 Michele Lanci-Altomare

Text Copyright © 2000 by BowTie ™ Press
Photographs © Gabrielle Boiselle

Library of Congress Cataloging-in-Publication Data

Of women and horses : essays by various horsewomen / commentary
by GaWaNi Pony Boy, author of Horse, follow closely ;
illustrations by various artists ; photographs by Gabrielle
Boiselle.
    p. cm.
"A GaWaNi Pony Boy book."
 ISBN 1-889540-52-8 (hardcover : alk. paper)
 1. Horsemen and horsewomen--Psychology. 2.
Horses--Psychological aspects. 3. Human-animal relationships.
I. Pony Boy, GaWaNi, 1965- II. Boiselle, Gabrielle.
 SF284.5 .O45 2000
 636.1'001'9--dc21

00-008922

BowTie ™ Press
A Division of Fancy Publications
3 Burroughs
Irvine, California 92618

Printed and Bound in Singapore
10 9 8 7 6 5 4 3

*This book is dedicated
to Riana and her love of horses.*

*I would like to gratefully acknowledge
all of the women in this book who have contributed to
changing the way we perceive and understand the horse.
I would also like to give special thanks to
Ruth Strother (the world's greatest editor)
and to Nick Clemente for his wisdom and insight.
I thank God for all of the blessings and
opportunities He has given me.*

—GaWaNi Pony Boy

Contents

Introduction

A strange stillness dwells
In the eye of the horse,
A composure that appears
To regard the world from
A measured distance…
It is a gaze from the depths
Of a dream…

— Hans-Heinrich Isenbart

An examination of these words almost diminishes their value.
Yet, the strange stillness that Isenbart speaks of draws me. I have a strong desire to be within this perfect circle of stillness. I believe that it is this calm, this clarity that draws us all, especially women, to the horse. Perhaps the glassy depth of the horse's eye provides a glimpse of the things we desire in our own lives. Horses are much like poetry in their grace, strength, rhythm, and time. I sometimes find it hard to analyze a horse's foot placement or conformation because I have a tendency to be entrapped by the beauty of all that is Horse.

Throughout my life, there have been several occasions in which I found myself in awe of that which exists between women and horses. It is more than a relationship, more than an attraction. This thing is undeniable, even indescribable. Are women attracted to horses or is it the other way around? Is there really something special between women and horses or is this a mere extenuation of the horse-crazy phenomenon experienced by both daughters and parents throughout the world? Do women have an innate gift that allows them to commune with our equine brothers and sisters?

Many times, when I was younger, I would take to the woods in search of some small stretch of stream that I had not yet explored. Time would stop, the world as my parents knew it would cease to exist, and I would be on my way. I always managed to come upon an unexplored portion of the stream. Even previously cataloged sections could be changed by heavy rainfall or a fallen tree. My purpose was pure and simple: to find and collect things. Snakes, rocks, peculiar-looking sticks, pieces of glass polished by the stream, muskrat, railroad spikes, horseshoes, a wounded goose, fossils, and any other thing that I felt had the need to be collected. And I collected them all.

Never did I carry a time-keeping device of any sort. Carrying a watch would strip me of my only excuse, ignorance, for not being home on time. I viewed my outings as explorations, but now I understand that they were anything but that. Like Christopher Columbus, Hernando de Soto, Ponce de León, or any other explorer, the object of my treks was to collect as many things as I could carry and bring home. Unlike Columbus, however, I did not get to keep them. Invariably, I was forced to return most of these things to "the exact spot" I had found them. My objective was not to take in new and exciting experiences but rather to take home *new and exciting experiences.*

Being the goal-oriented, hunter-gatherer, conquering type that I am—in other words, male—my mission was clear. Go out, find, collect, and bring everything home so that the entire family could share in the spoils. I did not know at the time that parents did not view dusky salamanders, dead trout, or old bricks as the coolest looking things on earth.

It never dawned on me that it was not necessary to obtain that which was the object of my attention. Nothing felt more natural than to observe something odd or special and then pick it up and possess it, at least for a little while. These were not explorations but rather they were small battles in which the person with the most things in his pockets won and the things lost.

I finally got over the need to conquer and collect (a few years ago), which brings me to the objective of this book: there is none. This book is an exploration. It is a journey. While speaking to the women who contributed their thoughts and ideas, I always mentioned that I did not intend this to be a conclusive work. I was not searching for answers and, in fact, did not know if there were any answers that we humans could comprehend. I was sure that I would be thought of as odd for exploring a subject without needing to come to a conclusion, but after speaking with just a few of these women I found just the opposite. This idea was not new or foreign to any of them. In fact, this more feminine way of processing data is what they are really good at. Later, my female peers bestowed upon me the highly coveted Now You're Getting It *award; an award rarely given to humans of my sex.*

Early on, I had concluded that I could not write about a subject that I could never completely identify with. I could appreciate the relationship between women and horses, and I could understand it somewhat, but I could never really be in the relationship. Rather than pretend to understand, I called on the help of my female peers. On the following pages are the thoughts and ideas of women whom I view as some of the most respected in the horse industry.

There was some skepticism, of course. "Why is a man writing a book about women and horses?" one horsewoman asked me during an interview. This question caught me off guard. After fumbling around with a few answers about objectivity and being a neutral moderator, the answer was given to me. I have—and have always had—a sincere interest in the subject. Because horses are patient teachers, I have come to understand them. I can understand the relationship between men and horses. Nevertheless, I have yet to understand the bond between women and horses.

So you actually want to know all those thoughts I've had for most of my life that no one has ever asked about or cared to listen to? *was a common response from many of the women included in this book. The knowledge contained in the following essays seems to have been hidden from society by the shroud of indifference. The women in this book have offered their patient teaching so that you and I might better understand that which is of women and horses.*

A WOMAN'S METAMORPHOSIS WITH HORSES

by Heather E. Greaves

You cannot remain unmoved by the gentleness and confor-mation of a well-bred and well-trained horse—more than a thousand pounds of big-boned, well-muscled animal, slick of coat and sweet of smell, obedient and mannerly, and yet forever a menace with its innocent power and ineradicable inclination to seek refuge in flight, and always a burden with its need to be fed, wormed, and shod, with its liability to cuts and infections, to laming and heaves. But when it greets you with a nicker, nuzzles your chest, and regards you with a large and liquid eye, the question of where you want to be and what you want to do has been answered.

—Albert Borgmann, *Crossing the Postmodern Divide*, 1992

When I first read this excerpt from Albert Borgman, I wept, and I still weep to this day whenever I read it. It brings to mind every horse I have come in contact with from the big, gray Thoroughbred lesson horse my first riding instructor saved from the slaughter sales, to the quarter horse who carried me through years of northern California shows, to the ponies involved in my master's degree research. How I feel when I see horses—as a woman, specifically—is difficult to describe: passionate, captivated, challenged, enamored, empowered, focused, overwhelmed, free. Their power and beauty touch my soul.

Women have changing relationships with horses. As we grow and change, so do our friendships. As children, the authority of the horse captures our wonder. My first mare was my caretaker: a strong, willing companion always ready for a long Saturday ride in the California foothills. I was the innocent and she the all-knowing. As teenagers, our horses become security and comfort. Later, as we swim around trying to find ourselves, we hop on Old Reliable's back and we know who we are. For some young women, horses become a substitute for boys, who appear to be too much of a risk. As we mature into our twenties, some of us replace this virile figure with a man, abandoning horses, while some make horses a more permanent part of our lives. By then, we have more patience and persistence, and working with our horses becomes more of a challenge.

When I work with my Thoroughbred, I not only feel challenged but I'm also completely focused. Whatever other problems I'm dealing with disappear for an hour or two. In this way, riding becomes my break from reality, a time when I know why I am. Somehow, this focus allows my mind to sort out other situations while I'm not even thinking about them. This is true for many women.

As women unfold into our thirties, our connection with horses develops into a shared relationship with children. As we have children, we are able to pass on to them our love for horses. It gives us precious time with our children in the hectic world in which we live.

Instinctually, women are caretakers, so it is natural for us to want to care for our aging companions. Once I settled in Florida, I sent for my beloved first mare, a quarter horse named Sweet Bid, so I could take care of her the way she had taken care of me. Now that Sweet Bid is twenty-three, I see her

in a different light. I am no longer the innocent and she the all-knowing. Now the roles have been reversed. Just as with our parents, we become the willing caretakers in our horses' old age.

Not only does our connection to horses change with age but our encounters with them influence our direction in life. When I see Sweet Bid, I feel the warmth and companionship of all the years she took care of me and the gratitude for the things she taught me. When I look at my Thoroughbred, Toccata, I see fire and grace and I'm compelled to tame the wild heart. Likewise, the ponies I worked with during my master's research remind me of people, each having his or her own quirky personality that I had to learn to work around. Each one of these horses is an individual who has impacted my life and will continue to do so.

Some people say women experience a relationship with horses because we see the horse as an equal, someone we can trust. I can't explain, except to say I feel I understand and appreciate the trust a horse or pony places in me. Maybe it is this relinquishing of power that women respond to and identify with. I know it puts a tear in my eye when such a powerful beast allows me to jump on its back with no saddle or bridle and ride around a pasture on a cold clear night under the stars.

My own experience with the horse has come about because of the influence of my grandfather, Otto Ferguson, and my mother, Susan Greaves. They steered me heavily in the direction of horses and I willingly followed. Therefore, it comes as no surprise that horses have encompassed every aspect of my life. Not only do I own, ride, and baby my horses but also I work with them as a career. Once, horses were only a recreation to me, a time to enjoy their company, or a quiet companion. With the passing of the years and the inquiries of adults about what I was going to do when I grew up, I insisted that I was going to raise and train horses. However, I had little idea how I was going to reach that dream. Years later, I operate Florida's premier embryo transfer recipient herd with my business partner, Vasiliki Meisenburg. Together, "Vickie" and I enjoy the grace and beauty of the horse on and off the job. I finally have my horse farm and can enjoy some free time with my own horses.

Perhaps because I am a woman, the hardest thing about having a horse business is to see these horses as just a means to money. I never will. Luckily, my occupation accommodates this business faux pas of mine. Our surrogate mares are individuals we know well. Our mares can be returned to us year after year. It is like bringing home an old friend, and we like this personal relationship with our charges.

I respect the grace and the willingness of the individuals of this majestic species. The power they hold, that they allow the trainer to shape and mold, has gripped my soul. I will always be enthralled by the horse.

God forbid that I should go to any heaven in which there are no horses.

—Robert B. Cunningham, 1917

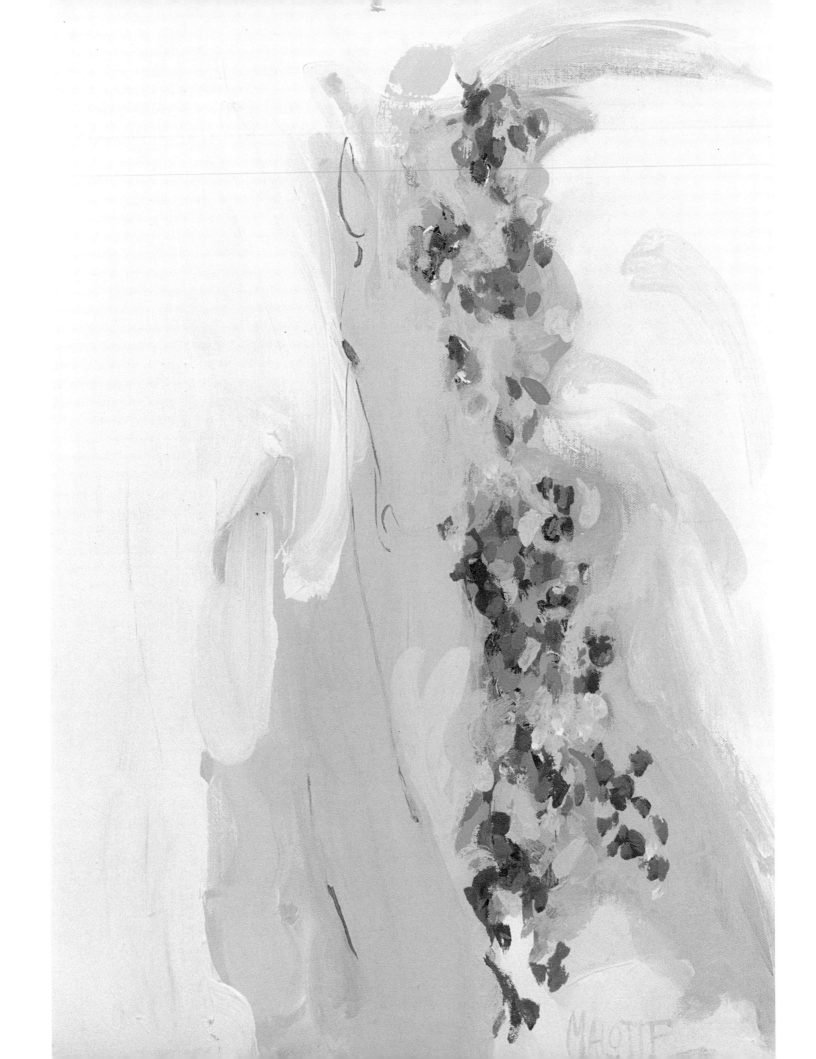

UNEXPECTED PACKAGES:
LESSONS FROM A SPECIAL HORSE

by Dr. Pamela L. Hamilton

Riding turns
"I wish"
into
"I can."

—Pam Brown

Most lessons
in life come in unexpected packages and in unexplained terms. Mine came in the form of a stubby rose gray Arabian colt.

I first met "Claire" (short for Benchmark Clarion) on his second birthday. It was a bitter cold, snowy February morning in rural Michigan. Claire was too much to handle for his owner. Though the colt had been shown extensively as a weanling and yearling, his personality was too surly to allow him to be a legitimate contender in halter classes. I bought Claire on the spot for $300. He was to be my next moneymaking project.

A college student always in need of funds, I reasoned that I would put thirty days of saddle training on him and then sell him at a significant profit to pay for my next semester of classes. When that time came, I could have sold him for a handsome profit. Instead, I decided to keep him for an extra thirty days to make an even greater profit. Nineteen and a half years and hundreds of blue ribbons and memories later, my sixty-day "investment" died in my arms of old age. Oh what I learned from his life and death.

I am not sure when I made the decision to keep the rose gray colt. I'm not even sure if I made the decision. After all, do we really decide who our best friends will be in the journey called life? Eventually I changed Claire's name to Falah. Only in retrospect have I realized how he truly was my benchmark in life.

I was, by nature, a tentative, cautious, reflective individual. I barely skimmed the surface of life; too shy, too afraid to dig deep into living. I was the quiet one; not confident enough to run, jump, or shout for fear of calling attention to myself.

I always sought to keep a low profile. However intellectually competent I was, I stood on the outside of academic accolades. However lonesome, I stood on the edge of social circles. However proficient in the show ring, I got "the gate" far more often than the glory.

Falah never afforded me the luxury of being tentative. In fact, the last time I was tentative, I ended up with a trip to the emergency room to set a fractured clavicle; a result of Falah's impromptu—albeit well placed—reminder to pay attention.

My major of psychology aided the training process. Keenly aware of positive and negative reinforcers, schedules of reinforcers, structuring the environment, and so forth, I was pleased by Falah's positive response to the training procedures. However, his disposition was not entirely endearing. In fact, he would pin back his ears and wrinkle up his nose in disgust every time I walked past his stall unless, of course, I had something tasty in my pocket. Not one for physical affection, he would succumb to the pleasures of peppermints. Unlike my other horses, I had to work hard at earning his respect.

The first time I won a blue ribbon was on Falah's back. I was nineteen years old as he deftly escorted me around the show ring as if he knew his purpose in my life. Falah taught me all the lessons other instructors had failed to get across.

"Sit up straight."

"Ride with your whole body."

"Put more effort into your riding."

"Pay attention."

"Look as if you're on the best horse in the world."

"Be proud"

Falah and I were undefeated for several seasons. Yet I never became complacent, partly because of his antics in the make-up arena. Invariably, he would turn in a lackluster performance: a mediocre park trot, a sprawled out canter, maybe a rein back, maybe not. I could feel the stares from fellow competitors, silently discounting us from the competition that day.

In the split second while moving from the make-up to the show arena, Falah transformed himself. The 14.3-hand dappled gray gelding became my knight in shining armor, ready to defend my equestrian honor. With purposeful cadence and rhythmic discipline, he moved through the paces to take his rightful place in the

winner's circle. I think Falah enjoyed playing mind games.

Our show career was long and lucrative. Lucrative not so much concerning finances (let's face it, we live our lives with horses because we love them, not because of the money) but concerning my personal growth. Falah's confidence begot my confidence. I learned to enjoy the success and attention that Falah and I garnered in the show ring. My newly discovered confidence began to affect other areas of my life. Grades improved because I participated more in class, relationships blossomed, and risks were taken. I was published in a national publication with an article titled "College and a Horse."

During the heyday of our competitive years, we were invited to join Chuck Grant's famed Horse Capades. Mr. Grant, the gentleman who helped dressage flourish in the United States, was taken aback by Falah's talents not only as a saddle seat and dressage horse but as a trick horse as well. His then silvery coat sparkled in the spotlights.

From the Horse Capades, Falah and I landed a stint at the Kentucky Horse Park acting as official hosts of the park to visiting guests, celebrities, and dignitaries. Again, Falah taught me valuable lessons. Falah was always so nonplussed about the fuss and attention devoted to him or surrounding celebrities. In fact, he once sneezed all over the flowing white garment of an Arabian sheik who had extended his hand in his enthusiasm to see an Arabian horse.

Falah taught me never to let status get in the way. In spite of his celebrity position, Falah felt no shame as he stuck his nose in ladies' handbags in search of a peppermint. No other adult could ride him, but he allowed hundreds of children to sit on him for vacation photographs.

One of my most cherished memories was at a time when Falah was the featured attraction at the Kentucky Horse Park. After the performance, applause, purse-rifling, and photographs, I turned Falah loose in the paddock area. The crowds had vanished and I turned my attention to putting away the props. I glanced over my shoulder to see Falah leaning over the fence gently nuzzling a solitary woman in a wheelchair, unable to reach out to touch him. Falah had reached out to her. The woman's misty eyes caught mine. The tears embarrassed her. She explained she had never touched a horse before, and in touching Falah, a dream had come true. In spite of all the accolades we collected, I shall always remember the tenderness of that singular moment when I saw Falah's heart turn to gold.

Times and circumstances passed, but Falah's friendship and loyalty prevailed. In spite of all the changes my young adulthood ushered in—getting married; moving away from my family; having a son, then a daughter; graduate school; a career; moving across the country—Falah was my one constant. He was a touchstone, a benchmark with which to measure my growth against who I used to be. Psychologists say that young adulthood is the loneliest time for women, and I suppose that would have been true for me if not for my relationship with Falah. My singular identity had evolved into a variety of roles: wife, mother, adult, psychologist, and community volunteer. When I was with Falah, however, I regained my center: unpretentious, down-to-earth, capable. I called my time with him my Falah fix. Falah christened our new barn by being the first to enter the threshold.

In spite of loving care and constant companionship, Falah grew old. Imperceptibly at first, yet steadily, Falah's life was coming to an end. I worried about the loss of dignity he might endure. I worried about the pain he might suffer. I worried that he might die alone, that I would not be there for him. I learned not to expect tomorrow. I learned to cherish the moments that make up a day. I learned to fully enjoy.

All along, Falah had taught me to get involved with life, even when life gets scary. So instead of shying away from the prospect of Falah's death to avoid personal pain, I relished my days with him. He filled up my senses: his earthly scent, his silky mane, the way he still crinkled up his nose when I ran out of carrots or peppermints. I found relief from the dread of his eventual death by living life fully. Living life fully helps me choose not to regret. I have learned to appreciate all that each new day brings. Simple joys abound if we look for them.

When Falah's last day arrived, I felt prepared: no regrets, be brave, be strong, help him pass through this life. Faithful friend to the end. Dawn came and went and gave way to the afternoon sun. Falah's silver coat glistened in the sun, shining, silky, reminiscent of his horse show glory days. Evening approached, the night as big and as dark as Falah's loving eyes. I vowed to stay with him. With death imminent, Falah walked out of his stall and circled the paddock area, as if to take everything in one last time: the gentle midnight breezes, the reflection of the moon in his water bucket, the soft sand under his hooves. He gazed up toward the house where my family slept, respecting and honoring our privacy and precious time alone.

Profoundly, I walked with Falah back into our barn. As if speaking a silent equine language, Falah lingered by each one of the other horses' stalls. Instead of the usual squeals and stomping when a horse has invaded another's territory, there was only silence. Falah gently touched the noses of his stable mates and returned to his stall. A brief nuzzle with his uncrinkled nose to my wet cheek, one last glance out his window to see the star-filled balmy night, and then he left me.

I cried for days; unashamed, unabashed, truly good cleansing cries. Not one tear was of regret but rather deep sorrow and grief over my best friend's absence. Falah is buried in the paddock where we spent so much time together. I don't grieve for him anymore, although I still miss him. But Falah taught me how to live life, and I enjoy so much of what life has to offer because of those lessons learned. It has been a few years since Falah died, but still on a taxing day, I will go out and sit by his grave. Warm images of happy times wash over me.

On the anniversary of his death, I carefully take out a big book filled with happy memories, my engagement photographs, my delicate lace wedding dress, the little light blue suit and pink rosebud dress my babies wore home from the hospital, and Falah's royal blue halter.

Some people say there are no animals in heaven, but I know differently. The book of Revelation speaks of "…heaven standing open and before me was a white horse, whose rider is faithful and true." When I get there, I will hug my old friend once again.

Yes, that is heaven.

Most theologians agree that animals do not have souls. I believe they do. I do not believe that they have the same sort of soul that we have, but nonetheless I believe that they have souls. The well-documented acts of horses reaching out to those in need amaze me. On several occasions, I have caught a glimpse of my horse Kola's soul. As Falah did for Dr. Hamilton, Kola has brought tears to my eyes more than once.

Kola is a good horse. He does his job well, but he is not without personality. When I have had little time to ride, Kola has exhibited his desire to get back to the barn, not in the normal barn-sour behavior, but in a calculating, manipulative behavior. He pins his ears, snorts, pounds his feet into the earth with each step—his entire body language telling me he is not a happy camper. He has dumped several friends of mine simply to get out of a leisurely trail ride. His size and conformation are that of a pony and so is his personality.

Yet even on Kola's worst day, I can put any child on his back and Kola will watch over that child with the gentleness and love of a grandmother. Kola has endured up to forty-five minutes being tugged by handicapped children. He has had his whiskers pulled by infants, his eye poked by toddlers, and his ears grabbed by six year olds, and he has never flinched. He has also exhibited great respect for elders. If you are above the age of seventy you can surely tug on Kola and be safe from rebuke. Kola's heart is a big one for those who need it.

What is the heart that our horses show us from time to time? Is it simply that we see what appears to be a human attribute and identify with it? Do we simply anthropomorphize the horse, projecting human qualities onto him? I don't think so. I have seen far too many examples of horses giving more than was necessary to discount their behavior. If any animal has the ability to touch our own souls, I believe the horse is that animal.

HORSES:
EXPRESSIONS OF OURSELVES

A Conversation between GaWaNi Pony Boy and Jane Savoie

A horse is the projection of people's dreams
about themselves—
strong, powerful, beautiful—
and it has the capability of giving us escape
from our mundane existence.

—Pam Brown

Jane is a really great gal.

I don't use the word *gal* often, but I think it's appropriate when describing Jane. She is humble, funny, down-to-earth, sincere, and sensitive.

These are not words that first come to mind when I think of an international rider, let alone an international dressage rider. But from the minute I met her, she seemed like the kind of person anyone would like to spend time with sitting around a fire and drinking hot chocolate. I could go on and on and on about her accomplishments in the equine world. But to me the real value is not in what Jane Savoie has done, but rather in who she is.

Before we got together for this interview, Jane had done some thinking about the special relationship she has with horses. She found that it's similar to an affinity she has for animals overall.

"I think I have an incredible rapport with dogs and horses, but, basically, I have a connection with all animals," she told me. "When I watch animals just doing their thing, I am filled with such a sense of wonder." She was looking out the window as we spoke and spotted her dog. The dog had caught the scent of something and stood still with her nose in the air, being totally in the moment. Jane watched the dog sniffing the air, and as she tried to describe it to me, she was filled with joy. "I can't explain it," she said. But I understood completely.

"When I turn my horse out, he has this ritual he goes through everyday," she went on happily. "He gallops across this huge field with broodmares and babies in the surrounding fields. Even though he's a gelding, he thinks they're all his." She laughs at the thought. "First, he gallops across. Then he passages like he's showing off for them. I can hardly tear myself away. I watch him interact with the other animals, and I just love that."

Jane clearly identifies with her horse taking off across the pasture like that. She says that if she were reincarnated, she'd probably come back as a Thoroughbred. "I'm high-strung, I'm high energy, I'm very, very eager to please. I will turn myself inside out trying to do whatever it is that I need to do. I think both the negative (if you want to perceive them as negative) and the positive aspects of a Thoroughbred sum up my nature and personality. Maybe that's part of the identification."

Jane does a lot of her training through mental pictures. "Of course, I do use aids when training," she added. "I teach aids to my horse and use those signals so that we can communicate nonverbally. But I also have a deeper level of nonverbal communication with my animals, which is basically mental pictures." I believe, as Jane does, that mental pictures are some of the things that animals understand best.

"I have to tell you what I did one day," she said. "I was staying with a friend who had a three- or four-year-old Doberman pinscher. This dog was totally unruly. While she was at work, my friend left her dog alone all day and the house was always torn apart when she returned. The dog would tear everything from the sofa's cushions to my friend's shoes. The dog didn't even know basic commands such as *sit* or *stay*. In a word, she was a hellion.

"I stayed with this woman while I was working with a trainer in Connecticut. One day, my friend went to work and I thought I'd experiment with this dog by trying to communicate with her through mental pictures. In two hours the dog learned to respond to the commands *come, sit, lie down,* and *stay*. We practiced over and over again and then when my friend came home, we showed her what we'd learned. From the other room, I called the dog with my mind, and she came bounding down the hallway. Then, without a single verbal command, I stopped her in her tracks and asked her to sit, stay, and lie down. This is similar to how I train my horses. I think it's fascinating, and I love having this level of communication with the animals I train."

I recognized what Jane was talking about. I tell people all the time that this is the language that Olympic competitors use, and most of them don't know how they learned it. When we set out to learn this language, we get a lot further with our animals more quickly.

It is accepted among dressage riders that the discipline attracts the artistic mentality. "As a group they are artistic and creative," Jane observed. "A lot of my friends who ride are painters, illustrators, or musicians. For the longest time I thought that I didn't really do anything creative. I wished that I could paint or dance or play an instrument like my friends were able to do. I never felt that I had the ability or talent to do those things. But you know, I finally realized that riding really is a creative outlet for me. I think of it as a living art form."

As an artist in the medium of horses, Jane loves riding into an arena that has just been raked—a pristine, level, smooth "canvas" just waiting for her to perform on.

"Going into an arena that has just been groomed, I get a feeling like figure skaters must get when they step onto freshly groomed ice. That arena is like a blank canvas to me and my horse. With my horse, I am creating living art—a dance— and it is incredible. It is a very personal thing but it is fulfilling to my creative side. I suppose I could try

to sing and dance but you definitely wouldn't want to hear me sing and you'd probably be embarrassed if you watched me dance!" She laughed.

"I like to think of my riding and training as part sculpting and part physical therapy," Jane observed. "I start with a horse who has a certain configuration of muscling, a certain amount of strength, a certain look. I then mold, sculpt, and redefine his body through the kind of work that we do in dressage. I love seeing the muscles start to bloom and the whole shape of the horse change. As my horse's physical therapist, I look at him and evaluate where he is weak, locked, blocked, or stiff. I then devise different physical therapy exercises so that I can strengthen, unlock, unblock, or loosen the horse where he needs it. My aim is for the horse to be more comfortable and, equally important, for

him to develop as an athlete. All of these changes to my horse's body contribute to my wonder. While I groom my horse, I notice his strong hindquarters and well-developed topline and take great pride that all of his conditioning is natural and brought about by correct training. None of it can be attributed to artificial means such as steroids or drugs."

As an example, Jane talked about one of her favorite horses. She got him from Holland six years ago and "he's a very odd-shaped horse," she said. "He's probably got the longest back I've seen. He's rangy in his frame and he didn't have much muscle at all when I got him. A lot of people laughed at the horse and commented about how ugly he was. I even heard rumors from Holland. Certain dealers were saying, 'I can't believe Jane Savoie bought that big ugly cow.' It was a big joke. A year later, I competed with this horse and the overwhelming comment I heard was something like, 'Oh my gosh, this horse is so beautiful. He's magnificent.' After a year of training, he had become strong and he moved like a dancer. He was beautiful to watch and only a year earlier everyone was laughing at him. It was rewarding to have lived up to one of the goals of dressage, which is that when the training is correct, the horse always becomes more beautiful."

Horses are a form of expression for riders—as painting or sculpting is for artists—but they're also a mirror, as Jane had discovered. While she was working on one of her books, the project brought into sharp focus what she has gained by having one particular horse in her life.

"It [the book] made me think about the horse I had for the Olympics in Barcelona when I was a reserve rider for the USET's (United States Equestrian Team's) dressage squad," she remarked.

"When I got him, I thought that he was the most wonderful, fabulous horse I have ever had. I was confused and disappointed when people I really admired and respected would say unkind things about this horse. One woman who was a knowledgeable international rider said, 'He's a naughty, disobedient piece of doo-doo.' I was dumbfounded by this comment. The next person I talked to also had impressive credentials. She said, 'This horse is totally taking advantage of you. He's a total bull.' And once again I was scratching my head. I had only had him for a couple of months—I really didn't know him all that well. These were people whom I admired and respected saying horrible things about him, and I just couldn't see it.

"I went to a friend who knew both riders, and told her that I was confused. I loved this horse. I thought he was really sensitive; he tried his heart out and everyone was telling me that he was terrible. 'Am I being completely naive about him?' I asked her. This woman is very wise. She said, 'Our horses are mirrors of ourselves. They are expressions of us. We both know and respect the two people you just spoke to. But let's face it, one is a really tough cookie and the other is a bit bullish. They see their own personalities in this animal. You feel that this is a horse who would turn himself inside out to please you, and you know that's how you are, Jane.' I learned from my friend that horses are merely reflections of who we really are. Once I realized that, I saw how much I could learn from my horses and how they provided me with a lot of opportunities for personal growth.

With this perspective—that horses are reflections of ourselves and that they're artistic expressions—I asked Jane why she thought that girls and

women are drawn to horses, of all the animals that they could identify with. Her answer? Beauty.

"I think about how limited my exposure to horses was—primarily for financial reasons—when I was little. I remember going to a fair when I was eight or nine years old. One of the games at the fair was the one where you knock over the milk bottles and one of the prizes was a little plastic horse about three inches tall. There were light blue horses and light pink horses and I was able to win five or six of them. I would play with them, put them in their little stable, and simply admire them. I remember thinking, *This is the most beautiful animal that I have ever seen*. They were just so beautiful and I still remember them that way. Almost every little girl I know falls in love with horses. Now that I'm a professional, the magic and awe of their beauty is still there.

"When I compete, there are two interesting things that happen to me when all is going well. The first is that I am totally focused and oblivious to my surroundings. I remember once at a competition in Florida, someone came up to me after my test. 'We were worried that you'd be distracted,' the person said, 'because one of the managers drove his golf cart right down the side of the arena with his backup beeper going off.' I hadn't even seen or heard him. That kind of tunnel vision happens often when I am really at one with my horse. The other thing that happens for me is that I experience a distortion of time where things happen in slow motion. I feel like I have all the time in the world to make adjustments and corrections. It's a glorious sensation that I enjoy as much as I enjoy being in my cocoon of concentration."

THE PSYCHOLOGY
OF WOMEN AND HORSES

by Delphi M. Toth, Ph.D.

If you have it, it is for life. It is a disease for which there is no cure. You will go on riding even after they have to haul you on to a comfortable wise old cob, with feet like inverted buckets and a back like a fireside chair...When I can't ride anymore, I shall still keep horses as long as I can hobble about with a bucket and a wheelbarrow. When I can't hobble, I shall roll my wheelchair out to the fence of the field where my horses graze, and watch them.

—Monica Dickens, the great-granddaughter of
author Charles Dickens, in her book, *Talking of Horses*

My great-grandmother

was impatient to go to the stable in the early morning, too impatient to waste time sorting left boot from right boot. Her riding boots were made so that the left and right boots were identical. She could shove her feet into the boots—left-right, right-left, no matter—and go quickly to what was really important: the horses. The lives of her horses and the perpetuation of her Hungarian warmblood clover lines were more important to her than material considerations, so important that she exchanged heirloom family jewelry for hay and oats during wartime in Europe. For many women, it is a given that horses are crucial to living life meaningfully and happily. Material and financial sacrifices are made willingly to keep horses in our lives.

Living in the city as a small child, I remember running to search for the rag man when I heard his chant accompanied by the distinctive clop-clop-clop-clop of his ancient gray horse's tired hooves. My grandmother would always retrieve me, scolding, "If you don't behave, I'll give you to the rag man." Rather than feeling fear, my child's mind thought this to be a rather good deal because I could then be with his wonderful horse all the time.

Every time I go into the barn now, I feel the same magic as I did when I was a child, looking up into big kind eyes and feeling the gentleness of a soft muzzle blowing warm, moist breath on my face. I continue to be enchanted and comforted by big, soft equine eyes and by that warm, velvety equine muzzle. I feel lucky that these magnificent creatures have given me their friendship.

It is undeniable that women have a special affinity with horses. Are there psychological reasons that women are drawn to horses? Yes. Are these reasons known within a degree of scientific certainty? No. As with the wind, we do not need to have scientific proof of its existence to know beyond a reasonable doubt that it is blowing.

In the beginnings of modern psychiatry, horses were regarded as symbols of sexuality and male power. Sigmund Freud used the relationship between horse and rider to help explain the relationship between the id (raw emotion, instinct) and the ego (reality, rational thought). The landscape of dreams is filled with images of rearing, galloping, charging equines, interpreted by psychoanalytic theorists as representations of sexual power. D. H. Lawrence, a literary doppelganger for Freud, wrote of the horse, "Far back, far back, in our dark soul the horse prances . . . The horse, the horse! The symbol of surging potency and power of movement, of action, in man."

In many cultures, prepubescent and adolescent girls are drawn strongly to horses. Using the interpretations of traditional psychoanalysts, this suggests that the interest in horses may represent early sexual feelings expressed symbolically. But the notion that a girl's fascination with and devotion to her horse is simply repressed sexuality is insulting both to the girl and to the horse. Children, especially female children, are fascinated by horses, images of horses, pretty ponies, rocking horses, pony rides, the unicorn, carousel horses, summer camp with horseback riding, and mechanical horses in front of the dime stores of the recent past. Horse figurines, calendars, books, and stuffed animals are popular even with children who have never seen a horse except on television or in movies. The horse-crazy girl is a well-known caricature in modern societies.

Men and women, in general, interact differently with horses, especially as children and young adults. The differences blur with age and experience with horses.

Men and boys enjoy primarily the power and speed of the horse. They want excitement and thrills when riding and use the horse as a toy or tool, an extension of themselves in their play, games, and contests. Many young males psychologically have a greater need for intense stimulation, the kind of sensory overload that strenuous, dangerous, adventurous activities provide; the concept of the high-sensation–seeking male is well recognized in psychology. Males seeking intense sensations become impatient then intolerant when forced to slow to the resting pace of the horse, and they move on to other activities. Motorcycles, dirt bikes, skateboards, in-line skates, and automobiles create fast-moving excitement that can serve the same purpose as horses for the young male.

Women and girls enjoy the power and speed of horses, but they also revel in the closeness of physical and emotional contact, and tend to seek an intense one-to-one relationship with the horse as a friend, as a confidant. Many boys ride, but it is girls who want to sleep in the barn with their horses and ponies, who spend countless hours grooming and pampering them, all the while talking to their equine friends about their secret feelings, hopes, fears, hurts. Many boys ride, but it is rare for a boy to spend all waking hours thinking about a special horse and all sleeping hours dreaming about horses, as girls often do. Boys' thoughts and dreams instead center on their own activities; the horse may be present but the horse is secondary to the action. In

these differing behaviors are hidden the fundamental contrast between men and horses vs. women and horses. For men, horses move them physically. For women, horses move them emotionally.

Many women and men, famous and unknown, have recognized the necessity for a close relationship with their horses for work or war or competition. But it is women who form such a close relationship routinely—almost automatically—not only with their work or competition horses but also with their backyard horses, with their boarded horses, or even with school horses at a riding academy. The desire for a relationship is what distinguishes the typical female horse person from the typical male horse person. It is the relationship with the horse that makes the female's experience with the horse so deeply satisfying, enjoyable, meaningful, and enduring.

A relationship with a horse is not identical to a relationship with another human. This does not imply that the horse-woman relationship is a lesser relationship, only that it is different. The quality of that relationship can be remarkable. Sometimes we long for relationships between humans to be so good. Let's look for a moment at what the woman brings to the relationship.

The little girl with her first horse or pony has enthusiastic unconditional childlike love for her big friend. She shares and plays with a horse or pony as she would a human friend or small pet: talking; role-playing; playing make-believe, fantasy games, and adventure games. Her horse may be her first best friend—a wonderful, tolerant playmate.

The adolescent girl brings more emotional needs to her relationship with a horse. She is feeling normal age-related insecurities, emotional turmoil, self-doubt, and intense self-consciousness. Her relationship with her horse is a contrast to the hypercritical world of adolescence and high school. She and her horse form a tiny clique characterized by unconditional and noncritical acceptance. The girl who feels unattractive, awkward, and unsure of herself becomes empowered and protected when with her beautiful, graceful, and sure-footed equine friend. Her ability to exert control over this powerful creature gives the adolescent girl confidence and a sense of accomplishment that generalizes to other parts of her life. The major developmental tasks of adolescence are forming an independent identity, beginning mature relationships, and obtaining education and training to begin the transition into the adult world. The horse prepares the adolescent girl emotionally to succeed in these tasks. The experience of a successful interaction with an equine ally may change the course of her life by increasing her self-confidence, self-esteem, assertiveness, and willingness to take on other difficult challenges.

The adult professional woman has varied needs. She may need to escape the demanding responsibilities of her work and spend time with an unquestioning friend who provides a few hours of calm in her hectic life. Barn tasks such as mucking a stall, cleaning tack, and grooming a dirty horse can be deeply satisfying. The woman can feel the joy of completing a real job, albeit a simple job, after a workday filled with loose ends, obstacles, unresolved problems, slow progress, and lack of appreciation. The absence of requests and demands, as well as the quiet environment of the horse barn, are relaxing and calming. Working in a barn can be equivalent to working out in a gym or spa, pumping hay and water rather than pumping iron, but the barn workout is more emotionally soothing and gratifying.

Increasingly busy professional and home lives cause women to lose touch with the rhythm of nature. Although this sounds trivial when compared with pressing work or family demands, the regular routine and pace of nature is beneficial psychologically and physically, as has been shown by numerous research studies. In taking on the responsibilities of caring for a horse, the woman is taking herself out of the home and out of the office or workplace, putting herself in the outdoors more, in natural light, away from buildings with controlled air and temperature. Exposure to natural light, especially during the winter months, is well known to prevent certain types of depression (such as Seasonal Affective Disorder). Going outside into the light every morning acts as a trigger, or zeitgeber, which resets the daily circadian clock, controlling chemical and hormonal body cycles. Trail rides or even riding in an outdoor arena demonstrate again the forgotten quality and beauty of each time of day and each season, providing the receptive mind with a renewed appreciation of nature.

Riding provides exhilarating and enjoyable physical activity and an opportunity for progress in the partnership of horse and rider. The joy of the ride is not only in the perfect toe position or completion of a pattern or test but also in successful communication with the horse, leading to paired harmonious movement—a dance. Again, it is the relationship with the horse that is central to the woman's experience of the horse.

Now let's explore what the horse brings to the relationship. Horses are honest and direct. Horses are nonjudgmental and without treachery. Horses think in straight lines; there is no dissembling, no deception. Horses are not impressed or embarrassed by superficial appearances—their own or their riders'. Horses, just as humans, are individuals; some sensitive and intelligent, some more dimly lit. But even the most unremarkable horse can literally and figuratively take you away from whatever you wish to escape—typically your current reality—at least briefly.

Horses are strong and powerful animals, easily capable of overwhelming a human. But they are also remarkably sensitive, vulnerable, and fragile. They are easily frightened and do not easily forget. The gentleness, sensitivity, and vulnerability of the horse may elicit nurturing in the caregiving woman. Women generally are more empathetic, more physically gentle than men, with softer voices and hands. This makes them initially less threatening to horses. The horse changes its human friend's behavior and attitude, softening, quieting, calming human responses. The horse is a sensitive sort of biofeedback monitor, picking up on subtle moods and thoughts. A tense person walking a horse makes the horse worried and vigilant. A tense rider conveys that tension to the horse, making it difficult for the horse to know what is being asked. In my psychology practice I have worked with competitive riders unable to handle their extreme stage fright or performance anxiety. Therapy involved training the riders to become calm and focused as needed so that their horses can do the job when asked. It is not necessary to do anything with the horse. Treat the rider and those distracting and confusing signals won't overwhelm intended communications.

In much of our lives, we must accept what is artificial, superficial, or trivial. But with the horse, women have the opportunity to encounter what is real, meaningful, and genuine, and to benefit emotionally and spiritually. You get out of a relationship with a horse what you are willing to put into it. The horse does not have the dishonesty or sociopathy to fail to reciprocate. This is not necessarily true of adult human relationships.

A puzzling aspect of the relationship between women and horses is that it is essentially a nonverbal relationship. Psychological research indicates that women are highly verbal and left-brain dominant. Women rely on words and verbal communication as their primary way to interact and understand. But with the horse, the woman is capable of developing an extended, intense caring relationship that is devoid of verbal conversation. This relationship is equivalent to a long, deep, intimate friendship between two humans who do not speak the same language but nonetheless communicate fully emotionally and physically; a pleasant fantasy but rarely reality.

In my work with couples in psychotherapy, it is common for the female partner to express frustration at the lack of verbal communication from her male partner. Yet with her horse, the woman sets aside her need for words of affirmation. In some cases, following referral for therapy with horses, women are better able to understand their human partners' nonverbal communication, leading to an improvement in the human relationship.

A fundamental tenet of psychology and psychotherapeutic practice is that the process is as important as the content. The process includes nonverbal communication, the overall context of the interrelationship, the intent of the individuals, the emotions of the individuals but not necessarily the words that are spewing out. In psychotherapy with a couple, it may be important to encourage the couple to focus on the process that is occurring, not the verbal content; to focus on the feelings, not the words; to focus on nonverbal communication, not verbal expression only; to communicate more as horses, not as noisy magpies endlessly chattering.

The horse is highly sensitive to sensory stimulation. Horses are not primarily verbal but instead communicate by means of sight, touch, smell, sound, rhythm, and kinesthetic cues, as well as more subtle messages. Communication with a horse is mental and intensely physical. The horse provides a pleasing symphony of sensory stimulation, all deeply gratifying to women. The horse provides calming physical sensations. Even the simplest acts of touching, petting, brushing an animal are calming to the human nervous and cardiovascular systems, as has been shown in numerous research studies. Women, especially, appear to benefit from sensory contact with the horse.

When mounted on a horse, we see the world differently, visually and psychologically. Being situated on a horse does not connote social ranking as it historically has, but literally being above others may increase feelings of pride and self-worth. One of the beneficial side effects of therapeutic riding is that it temporarily removes individuals from their wheelchairs—in which people literally look down on them—and moves them above everyone else, forcing others to look up to them for a change. All of my patients who use wheelchairs have commented on the metamorphosis in attitude that follows rising from the chair to the saddle.

The sounds of the barn are calming and subtle: the soft throaty nickering of the horses, the munching of hay, the slurping of mash, the swishing of tails, even the white noise buzzing of flies in the summer. The moving sounds of the horse's hooves mimic the lub-dub lub-dub rhythm of the human heartbeat. As such, these sounds calm us.

All horsewomen can conjure a memory of the lovely combination of leather, wood, straw, sawdust, fragrant hay, sweet feed, and the musky smell of the horse that signifies a horse barn. Smells comfort us, remind us of good times in our childhood. Humans disparage the role of smell in communication, yet we use perfumes and deodorizers obsessively. Smell is a primitive sensory system, based in the rhinencephalon (the olfactory part of the forebrain), and the sense of smell remains highly sensitive in humans, especially women. Tremendously strong emotional reactions can be generated by smells, especially familiar smells. Déjà vu is thought to be a response to a remembered smell; déjà vu is puzzling because the individual is searching for visual clues to explain the memory and can find none because the memory is based instead on smell.

Touch is an important means of communication and bonding for horses as well as for women. An excellent means for developing rapport with a horse is to give that horse a long leisurely deep grooming. The tactile and pressure sensations are calming to the horse and communicate the groom's friendly, caring intentions. Is there anyone who has not found the special tickle spot that causes a horse's lips to purse and tremble in exquisite delight and his or her body to contort to keep pressure on that spot?

Kinesthesia, or movement and rhythm, are feelings given to us intensely from horses. There is the exhilaration of rapid movement when riding as well as the comfortable feeling in the distinct rhythms of the gaits. The bouncing rhythm of the trot is akin to the bouncing of small children to burp them, then later in their lives to calm them when they are overactive. The rocking feeling of the canter is a fundamental rhythm, akin to the rocking given to babies in arms, rocking cribs, rocking horses, and rocking chairs. In severe trauma situations, such as earthquakes or war, humans often pull their arms tightly around themselves and rock back and forth for hours, unconsciously attempting to comfort themselves. I often work with patients to develop imagery that they can use to calm themselves. Grooming a horse has been one of the most successful relaxation images for women who have horses; it is kinesthetic, nonverbal imagery.

When riding a horse, we see nature differently, we have a different psychological perspective; we are not outside looking at nature, rather we are part of it. Just as the hot air balloon moves as one with the wind and the passengers feel no movement of air, when riding a horse we are one with nature, not moving against it. We become part of and attuned to a multitude of natural sensory stimuli.

The bottom line in thinking about the psychology of women and horses is to recognize that the relationship itself is important. The relationship between woman and horse provides a feeling of power and control without force, increased self-confidence, increased self-esteem, increased self-assurance. The relationship is characterized by reciprocated affection, unconditional acceptance, companionship, and accomplishment.

Horses are one of women's best-kept secrets. There is an immediate camaraderie with anyone else who rides. It is like a secret society. There is an instant network of friends around the world interested in the same breed or the same riding or driving discipline. Many women who board horses find an immediate circle of friends among the other female boarders, friends with many commonalties of interest.

We may not be able to put into words precisely what is important in the relationship between women and horses, but the failure to specify does not take anything away from the relationship. There is the subtle way in which movement changes around horses, the pleasant feeling of exhausted comfort that occurs after stable work, the feeling of incredi-ble joy in moving as one with a horse, thankfulness that as humans we are able to interrelate so closely with horses. Maybe when Freud and D. H. Lawrence were talking about the horse as a sexual symbol, they really meant that in relationships between women and horses, horses represent an asexual intimate bond. What if they had not been talking about sexuality, but emotional intimacy? Truly intimate emotional relationships are increasingly rare because of the multiple factors in our current world that pull people apart. When you look into your horse's eyes and that thousand-pound powerful and sensitive animal looks back at you with complete openness, a clear relationship exists. The horse's acceptance of you, as you really are, is a profoundly affirming psychological experience.

The dreamlike horse appeals to the psychologist in us all.
Yet it is his flesh and blood and thunder side, his rhythm and his power,
which brings us back to our roots, connecting us to Mother Earth.

—Sylvia Loch in
The Classical Rider: Being at One with Your Horse

After a day of work as a psychologist, I am sometimes emotionally and spiritually drained. When I arrive home and walk out to the barn, the horses call out and my exhaustion begins to fade. As I begin the familiar routines of horse care, I experience joy being with my equine friends who always provide an oasis of sanity in what seems at times to be a very disturbed and unnatural world. I am always filled with a sense of well-being, physically, emotionally, spiritually. Nothing else in my long life's experience has ever provided this sense of natural well-being except the horse. My favorite coffee mug, purchased at the local tack shop, summarizes my thoughts eloquently: *My horse is my therapy!*

Perhaps my favorite part of my job is the private evaluations with horses and their owners. In an evaluation I take a horse into a small training area and ask the horse to perform various simple tasks. What I'm really asking are questions. I might ask the horse to move forward, stand still while I touch him, give to pressure, or step over obstacles. The answers that the horse gives enable me to evaluate his attitude and personality. The horse also tells me how much training he has in different areas, what his previous teachers were like, where his strengths and weaknesses are, what he enjoys and what he doesn't. This isn't rocket science and it doesn't require learning a new language. From outside the training area this looks like nonverbal communication, but is it really?

Verbal means of, relating to, or associated with words. Webster's definition of word is "a unit of language comprised of one or more morphemes." My definition of verbal is the expression, written, spoken, or otherwise, of a complete concept. Although my definition of verbal communication may lie on the fringe of Webster's, I don't know that nonoral communication is any less verbal (expressing complete concepts) or effective than traditional verbal communication.

While making evaluations, my client (the human) might ask me, "What did that mean?" or "Why did she swish her tail right then?" or "Was that the lip thing you were talking about?" What I've noticed is that when most people try to understand their horses' language, they immediately turn to what we call body language; the movement or position of certain body parts in relation to the whole. Body language is a great start, but we can't rely solely on body position to receive communication from our horses. Just as with our own language in which words (expressions of a complete concepts) can have different meanings depending on context, timing, how they were said, and if they were indeed said to us, the language of the horse is complex but not in any way complicated.

If you ask your horse a question, expect an immediate answer. Perhaps the question is, "Will you move forward when I ask you to?" Your horse may answer yes by taking an immediate step forward. Your horse may answer no by doing nothing. Or, your horse may go into some lengthy explanation about how his previous trainer didn't acknowledge his answers so your horse just decides to start ignoring humans. Whatever your horse's answer is, it will be immediate and easily translatable. By asking and answering questions, we begin to develop a conversation with our horses. Conversation is an excellent way to get to know someone and in fact, it is our primary means of initiating and cultivating relationships. By being attentive to our horses' questions and responses, we can easily understand the language of the horse.

Remember that your horse is forever asking you questions and you are forever answering him. If you don't remember answering any of the questions that your horse has asked you, perhaps you should be worried about the answers that you gave without knowing that you did so.

THE HORSE AS GOD'S INSTRUMENT OF TEACHING

by Deborah Day

WORTH THE WAIT

I read every horse story written,
I drew horses on every paper in view,
I pranced around the yard with a rope on.
The horse was my milieu.

I dreamed of the day when a horse would be mine,
I built little stables of wood.
I begged my parents incessantly,
And saved all the money I could.

But marriage came first,
And then children, of course.
The years they actually flew.

And then one day the time was right;
I could buy my first horse, I knew.

She was an old buckskin mare,
Sturdy and sound, reliable, steady, and smart.

She carried me and I loved her,
I gave that old mare my heart.

—From Mares, Mud, and Manure by Nancy Callery

A few weeks ago, my mom sent me home with a box full of artwork I had created in elementary school. It was overwhelming to find that nearly every picture contained a horse, no matter what the theme. Each paper was signed, Debbie G. Horse. Later this week, I'm going back East for a wedding. I haven't been to Connecticut since I was a child, but I feel I must see the little converted carriage house where we lived and the stable (if it's still there) where I implored my mother to stop to let me see the horses. I am told that is when the horse craziness started. I was two years old.

In school, I was called the horse girl. I remember romping the playground like a horse, drawing horses into other kids' pictures for a cookie or whatever they had to offer, and standing at the trash cans after lunch collecting uneaten apples for my pony. In second grade, I broke both of my arms tripping over my "reins" while playing—the first of many of my equine-related casualties. Just the other day, a close friend declared that I'm part horse. She said that I'm too natural with them for it to be otherwise. I consider that a compliment of the highest sort.

Time and time again I have been asked not why I love horses but why I love them so much. What it is that has me polarized to horses is somewhat of a mystery even to me. This is my first organized attempt to explore my feelings for horses and to articulate my thoughts.

A few months ago, my old friend an Arabian gelding named Omar was put to sleep. He was my dream-come-true when I was thirteen and he was seven. We shared twenty years together, growing up, learning, training, showing, and traveling the country from Catalina Island to the Colorado Rockies. He was my confidant and friend through the tumultuous trial of youth and my faithful companion through all the changes since. He was an answer to my desperate prayers for a horse when finances wouldn't permit one and a tangible reminder that God is real in a personal way. Our companionship spanned most of my life. I find myself pondering our many experiences as I adjust to life without him.

I seem to have an elemental or visceral connection to horses. It's something that hasn't waned with maturity, marriage, childbearing, or even horse-related traumas. It is something unlearned and natural—but not quite tangible. I remember when my friend was killed from a fall off her horse. I was eleven, and she a little older. Many local kids stopped riding then; I couldn't. Three years ago, I was galloping a horse when he fell and rolled over me. For six months I was unable to ride. I was afraid of being afraid to ride, but when I could finally get back in the saddle it was just like old times.

I know that horses are not only a part of my life, they are an intrinsic part of me. My association with them touches all parts of my being: the emotional, the sensual, the spiritual, the intellectual. I feel at home when I am around them, whether cleaning their corrals, feeding, riding, painting, sculpting, or making the rounds before I go to bed. The aromas of manure, hay, leather, and sweat mingle together and follow me through the day. The horses' nickers, whinnies, and other welcome expressions edify my spirit. Care for them structures my days.

My perception of the world goes hand in hand with my association with horses. I marvel at the illuminated haystack in the morning sun—always a brilliant inspiration for a new day. In the evening when I feed them, the shadows are long as the horses mill around, stirring up dust. The sky is a golden glory—sometimes red, sometimes pink, often mottled with clouds in reverberating color. The purple and blue of the hills provide a luscious contrast as the sun slowly goes down behind them. I remember my days are numbered and sometimes stop to reflect on whether I've made this one count.

I love the chaparral that grows where I ride. Its beauty is subtle but full of life and vigor. There is a hill near our house that I ride to as often as I can. I hike to the top, leading my horse, where there is a large rock on which I sit. From there, my house is the size of a postage stamp, and the horses are like ants. I feel closest to God here. There are no distractions. Sometimes I read, sometimes I write in a journal, and other times I come just to be quiet. My horse is a beautiful black gelding. Here he grazes or drinks water poured into my hand. Sometimes he just stands and rests his chin on my shoulder. I feel refreshed and stronger for having these times.

My studio is nestled among corrals. I'm surrounded by a dozen or so horses: a cross section of breeds in a rainbow of equine colors. As I think about the horses in my life and those with whom I have worked in different places over the years,

I marvel at what they teach me. Horses are simple and honest. I have to be that way, too, to stay in touch with the important things of life. My tendency is toward the busy and complex. Horses remind me to be clear and concise. One must be quiet to hear them speak; so it is with people too. Horses learn from touch and voice. I earn their trust when I am calm and consistent. They respond to praise. I learn that temperance is essential.

There is no exhilaration equal to that of being astride such a powerful creature who has yielded to his rider and works in harmony with her as one. When I am aligned to my Maker in this sort of a way then I can best fulfill His purpose for me. I see the horse as an instrument by which God teaches me about life. Maybe it is the Creator himself who has placed this affinity for horses within me and maybe that is why I love them so much.

The first thing that horses have taught me is patience. When working with horses, one learns early that time does not exist; not in the mind of a horse, anyway. We tend to forget that the concept of time is one created by humans. With horses, there are rhythms to a day—feeding time, nap time, bedtime, waking time—everything in between is just life as a horse. This lack of structured time in a horse's mind makes things difficult for the rider or trainer. The horse does not know that you've been at it for three-and-a-half hours. The horse knows only that he has not yet been rewarded in the way that he's used to for a job well done. The horse knows that he has not yet successfully interpreted your language. The horse knows that you seem to be getting more frustrated and aggressive; but the horse does not know about this thing we call time. So we are left with two options. Either teach the horse to understand time (impossible) or forget that time exists. Now I suppose I could just say be really patient, but as long as you use a time reference in your training, your patience will never outlast the clock. Measure your horse's success not by how long it took for him to reach success but by how well he did.

The horse has also taught me what it means to be a horse. Although from a young age I worked with and for horse trainers, none of them was able or inclined to teach me what it meant to be a horse. It is important that if you are going to teach horses you must identify with horses—almost become a horse—and that requires an empathy that only a deep and abiding love can create.

The most important thing that horses have taught me is the difference between urgent and important. I am by no means a master of discerning the two, but horses have given me a few clues. Grass is important, water is important, rolling is important, and napping in the sun is very, very important. Most of the things that we humans do are urgent. If we could always complete the important before considering the urgent, we would be a relatively stress-free society. And if we chose the important over the urgent we would be a little closer to horses.

LIVING YOUR LOVE

by Mary Wanless

To be loved by a horse,
or by any animal,
should fill us with awe—
for we have not deserved it.

—Marion C. Garretty

As far as I am aware (and I have little historical knowledge), the love story between women and horses is predominately a twentieth-century phenomenon. But it is hard to believe that individual women did not have deeply significant relationships with their horses well before that time.

The last hundred years have seen the horse's role evolve from beast of burden and transport to that of family member. He now faces social instead of utilitarian tasks, and instead of having predominately male riders and handlers, his "significant others" are predominately female. Perhaps it took wealth and the changing social order of the post-World War II period for enough women to have enough contact with enough horses for us to reach some kind of critical mass, and for the concept of *horsey women* to become an entity. Perhaps it took film for this relationship to be glamorized and placed in the public domain as a phenomenon. Perhaps it took Freud to give us a psychoanalytic interpretation (from a male perspective, of course) that we could feel justified in rallying against.

Like a large percentage of women I meet around horses, I was in love with them from as early as I can remember. Living my fantasies of riding and being around horses took a very long time, but throughout those years the fantasy remained all-consuming. But at the age when so many little girls are goggling either real ponies or the ponies in their picture books, most little boys could not care less. They are besotted with engines and the need to put things together and take them apart.

Looking back, I think horses held such a magnetic attraction for me because of their beauty, grace, power, gentleness, and vulnerability, and because of the enormity of their spirits—spirits so bold and free, yet so willing to be tamed and trained. My horseyness began during early childhood, when my spirit, too, was being tamed and trained, learning the social skills and behaviors appropriate for a young girl in the culture of that time. They were hard lessons, and I suspect that I know, somewhere in the deepest recesses of my being, that they were costing me dearly. I was developing a social mask, an acceptable persona, and was losing access to my spirit and my core self. Horses, somehow, kept that spirit alive. They represented wholeness, the richness of my entire self, and they gave meaning to life. But this meaning would have so much more reality if only I could be with them more.

It is tempting to romanticize the relationship that women have with horses, and as much as some of us might think of women as all good and men as all bad, it is really not that simple. I often wonder if little boys, too, are searching for meaning when they feel compelled to take things apart, and if their search for wholeness just takes a different form. But when one's quest for wholeness requires a relationship, finding wholeness is not an easy task. Living your love in any close liaison becomes so very testing because everything that happens matters so much.

So whilst many women are extremely sloppy about their horses when they are off them, the agenda changes once they are on them. With riders of both sexes, the combination of high expectations and low skills marks the beginnings of stress for the horse. Low expectations and low skills can never be an ideal; but unless high expectations are matched with high skills and an extremely ethical philosophy of training, the horse suffers—he suffers more than he would from ignorance. For as the old classical masters of dressage used to say, "where art [skill] ends, violence begins."

Since women reach the limits of their skills just as often as men do, it is perhaps fortunate that we do not have as much weight to throw around as they do. In general, we have a lesser need to be right, to dominate, and to win at all costs. We're less likely to regard riding as a battle. But we still have our ambitions and our insecurities, and riding can trigger these emotions. A frightening number of horses are still forced to carry the burden of our ego needs. If a rider views a bad canter transition purely as a behavior, then to mess it up is no big deal. But if the rider progresses from "I rode a bad

transition" to "I can't find transitions" to "I'm having a bad day" to "I'm a bad rider" and ultimately to "I am a bad person," then every transition has the potential to prove that the rider is either good or bad. Ultimately, every step the horse takes becomes loaded with meaning. When that's the environment, God help the horse who puts a foot down wrong.

It might be a sweeping generalization to say that men have to prove they are dominant, whilst women have to prove they are good. But if our riding is the means for proving anything, we are using the horse in the service of the ego's needs, which are needs the horse should never have to fulfill. Even the love that many women give their horses is not given freely, for there is the expectation that the horses should love them in return and be grateful for their care. When a horse is required to love a woman more than he simply loves being a horse, he is in big trouble, for he can rarely live up to expectations. His love and loyalty would supposedly extend to being "good," so when he fails to act as required, he lets the woman down badly. Hence she feels that recriminations are in order. What she fails to realize is that she has made a one-way bargain, one that the horse never agreed to.

Among horse people, women as well as men, there are (to borrow from the language of transactional analysis) victims, rescuers, and persecutors. These roles are malleable, and victims can sometimes become persecutors, sizing up their opponents and snatching a chance to be one up instead of one down. This happens so commonly with people and their horses—especially when one is angry with one's spouse, mother, or boss—that I am tempted to say "let he who is without sin amongst you cast the first stone." Even rescuers are rarely as generous as they first appear for they seek hidden rewards. And when the rewards do not materialize, they, too, can become persecutors. Thus there are very few people who "level" with their horses, coming from a position in which neither party is perceived as inferior. But if our communication with our horses is going to foster mutual respect and be "clean" (not loaded with hidden agendas), we must have the skills that make it so. What so few people realize is that those skills are learned from the horse, and that he is our ultimate teacher.

It was undoubtedly men who created the expectation that horses should cross the great divide between our species and called them stupid when they did not. What these "trainers" never realized was that the human language is such a jumbled mass of contradictions to the horse that it makes no sense to him. But as much as we women might like to think ourselves as the saviors of the horse, we have to acknowledge that it has been men—the most forward thinking trainers of the American West—who have been the ones to right the wrongs between human and horse, showing the way to other riding cultures whose traditions have been less brutal.

It's sad to realize that so few riders—and even (though I hesitate to say it) so few women—have the humility to learn from the horse and thus to communicate with him in his own language. Whether you are on the ground or on his back; whether you are an ambitious, competitive, or backyard rider; I believe that you owe this understanding to your horse. Understanding and the ability to communicate with your horse, or your best efforts along this path, is living your love.

And there are so many choices now about how to do that. You can communicate with your horse through riding. You can become skillful at working him in a round pen or on the end of the longe line. Or you can learn the skills of touch, discovering how to read your horse's body and ease his aches and pains.

Meeting any of these challenges may require you to evolve and change both who you are and how you perceive yourself and your horse. One of my old teachers used to say, "The rider needs both sensitivity and authority, but it is so rare to find both of those in one person. If you are strong in one, you're lacking in the other." This might seem like the archetypal divide between men and women, and perhaps we are all in search of a wholeness that incorporates the strengths of both sexes. So it is that riding and handling horses can become a path of personal discovery. The less natural talent you have, the more you stand to learn—and to gain as a person—from your interactions with your horses.

And what of the theories of Freud? Whilst I like to think of riding as a path of physical, mental, emotional, and spiritual development, I can contemplate the possibility that he might have had a point. But I remain convinced that the longings of so many women to be around horses are primarily spiritual and not sexual in their nature. One of my pupils, however, once returned from a holiday in America, displaying a bumper sticker that read, "Put something exciting between your legs, ride a horse." Freud would have approved of that one!

Whilst it may be tempting to think of yourself as your horse's mom—especially given his dependence on you and the amount of his shit you will probably have to shovel—this is something of a sell-out, and you're not touching the entirety of your relationship with him. Riders who are more up-front willingly acknowledge that their horses have as much the role of their dancing partners as of their children. One young friend of mine, when she was complimented on being such a good mummy to her horse, responded firmly, "I am not his mummy. I am his girlfriend."

The relationship between many of us women and our horses is so close, exciting, demanding, and intimate, that it can be the most profound of our lives. So perhaps it is not surprising that several women I know once had husbands who had implemented the final solution to their marital problems. "It's me or the horse," they had announced, only to be told in no uncertain terms that the woman concerned would rather share life with her horse. My own ex-partner once declared indignantly, "I'm not like your horse, you know, you can't just shut me in a stable and forget about me!" Little did he realize that I rarely forgot about my horse, and never shut him in for very long. That man just didn't know his place.

After reading this piece by Mary Wanless, I decided that it would be impossible to get around the issue of male qualities vs. female qualities. Do horses know the difference? I believe they do.

Historically, among my people women cared for the horses and men used the horses. Women provided grooming, supervision, and love while men utilized the horses' abilities and attributes. It has been much the same throughout world history. While men were sitting atop wagons, bringing their goods to market, their daughters spent countless hours caring for, riding, drawing, dreaming about, loving, playing with, and admiring these beasts of burden. It seems to me that women have appreciated everything about the horse a little bit more than men have. It also seems that the horse respects those who understand him more than those who don't.

I have come upon an understanding that seems to hold true throughout the horse world. It isn't just a coincidence that the champion riders are those who seem to have a real understanding for the horse—not just an understanding of what the horse is, but a real identification with who the horse is. I have met and spoken to many champion male riders, who consistently give an outstanding performance in their discipline. To date, I have never met a champion who was also a jerk. I have a met a few fleeting stars who were far too egotistical to even talk to, but those men whom I consider champions are very nice people. As for trainers, I have never met a truly great male trainer who was egotistical or macho. Now I have met many macho male horse trainers and every one of them seems to have more problems with horses than is necessary; but the great male trainers that I have met are also really great people.

For example, I have a male friend who is a great horse trainer, probably among the top five in the United States. This man is sensitive, caring, soft-spoken, calm, has smiling eyes, and is generally a really nice guy. Sensitive, caring, soft-spoken, calm—we think of these qualities as feminine, don't we? Is it possible that horses respond better to men who are in touch with these feminine qualities as well?

And what about women? I don't know any great female riders or trainers who are pushovers. The great horsewomen that I know are strong, aggressive, demanding of respect, and what I would consider powerful. Aren't these qualities generally labeled as masculine?

I spend many hours throughout the year speaking about a subject that is vitally important to any rider of any discipline. I hold bareback clinics discussing and teaching this very subject. But never, until now, have I thought of this subject in quite this way. Balance. Balance is the most fundamental factor affecting how well you ride. Balance is what determines your ability to teach the horse within his own ability. And balance, it seems, is what the horse searches for in a human companion. The horse is strong and sensitive, aggressive and affectionate, powerful and graceful. The horse searches for a companion who mirrors his or her own personality. So to succeed with horses we must be like horses, and to be like horses we must be balanced.

BREEDING EXPERIENCE

by Terry Ventura

*Show me your horse
and I will tell you
what you are.*

—Old English saying

I'm watching my new saddle-bred mare, Missy, frolic in the pasture. This normally calm, complacent horse has turned into a schizophrenic in the past few days. She is alternately courting then screaming at and kicking the poor geldings on our ranch. It looks like a junior high school dance out there.

I call my vet, Darrell Zehrer, and tell him I think the time has come to order that shipment from Stallion Avenue. Darrell says he'll be over ASAP to evaluate the situation. I am new to this breeding business, so I figure I'm wrong, and Missy won't be ready, but after a thorough examination, Darrell says we have a follicle and to call George Haydon at Stallion Avenue right away.

I'm absolutely thrilled to call George. He is so funny and so calm about all this. I tell him it's urgent and to send the "stuff" right away. George says it will be on a plane in the morning. I'm to pick it up tomorrow at the airport—during evening rush hour!

A trip to the airport is never fun when you aren't going anywhere, especially when you have to drive approximately thirty miles through a lot of ticked-off people trying to get home from a rotten day at work. Also, I have to enlist the help of the husband. I ask him to drive me so I won't have to pay the $10 parking fee just to run in and pick up a package. Now, with the husband getting up at 4:30 A.M. to do a radio show, by 4:00 or 5:00 in the afternoon he is pretty darn tired. Lucky for me, he's is great sport and is almost as excited as I am for our first "pregnancy," so the trip isn't that bad.

Then I get to the airport. First I wander around the terminal (while my husband circles around the exterior), trying to find the correct pick-up counter. When I do find it, there are only one or

two people in line, so I am relieved. A couple of other people walk up to wait behind me. I get to the desk and a man asks my name. No problem, I tell him. "Where is the package from?" Again, no problem, and I answer. Then he says it. "What's in the package?" Presumably, they have to ask for security reasons. In a small room full of nonhorse people, I have to say what is in the darn package—to a man I don't know! I get red in the face and panic. Do I utter the scientific and not-too-offensive words *frozen semen?* Of course not. I blurt out "SPERM." The room cracks up, and the guys behind the counter try to remain calm and complete the paperwork so I can leave. I get in the car and I feel like a fool. My first really big chance to seem like a big-shot professional in the horse business and I blow it. Oh well, in the morning I will help the vet get this mare bred. I am so interested in the whole process. I always wanted to be a vet or work with one, but would never have had the guts to make the really heartbreaking decision vets face every day.

The morning comes, and I remember that I have promised to help with a big event at my daughter's school. "Well, this can't wait," the vet tells me. "Can Jesse help?" he asks. Again, I go to the husband and again, he is willing to help. I explain that all he has to do is hold the lead rope and let Darrell do the rest. My first mare is being bred and I won't even be home! I have to miss the whole thing and won't get to learn how it is done or ask any of the questions I planned to ask. The upside is that I have a wonderful day with my daughter.

When I arrive home, the mare is still a little quiet from the process. Jesse looks at me and says, "That was so disgusting! How can you watch that stuff and call it interesting? At what point did

Darrell decide he wanted to do that for a living?" But all I can think is that I missed it.

A couple weeks later, we get an ultrasound and a picture of our little one. It looks like a big black spot. We are so thrilled that we hang it in the barn office under a picture of his sire, Local Hero, clipped from the pages of *The National Horseman*.

Now comes eleven months of waiting and watching, worrying over Missy's every little change of mood or habit. Missy looks at me with gorgeous brown eyes, as if to say, *I've done this before, just relax*. She is even more calm and loving than ever. She rests her head on my shoulder and breathes softly on my neck, begging to have her ears scratched when I enter to feed or groom her or put her outside. All the usual pasture shenanigans seem to bore her, and she keeps to herself or hangs around Skyhawk. He has appointed himself as her guardian. Sky will not allow any other horses near her, and she tolerates his protective nature.

It's finally due date time—April 1—April Fools' Day. I hope this is not an omen. We had moved Missy to her foaling stall, filled with fluffy soft straw, about two weeks ago. One night, I set up a cot and battery-operated lantern, and slept in the stall with Missy. She tried to play with the lantern and begged me to scratch her head, then finally decided to go to sleep. She lay down next to my cot and groaned with her burden. Just as I started to drift off, Missy started to snore! I'm not talking loud breathing, I'm talking truck-driver-with-a-deviated-septum-and-bad-cold snoring. I get no sleep and no foal that night. My daughter, her friends, and her horse-loving cousin have been sleeping in the barn office and checking on the

mare for the past two days. School is out for spring break, and it's like summer camp.

It's now a week or so past the due date. I've since given up sleeping in the barn. The kids are back at school and on a regular schedule. I've taken to going out at 3:00 A.M. with a flashlight to check on Missy. It seems too cruel to walk into a dark barn and flip on all those lights. The horses' eyes would be blinking and looking dazed.

This particular night, it is very cold and I'm very tired. I lay in bed and try to decide if I should go out to the barn or stay in my nice warm bed. Suddenly, I hear a noise in the basement. A little concerned, I walk to the basement door and see light coming from underneath. We have walk-out doors to the yard, so now I am thinking along the lines of burglars in our home (Come on, it's 3:00 A.M., who else would be in our basement making noise?). I wake my husband, an ex-Navy Seal, with the words, "Honey, there's a burglar in our basement." What was I thinking? He leaps from the bed, throws on his pants, and gets his gun. We creep to the basement door and open it slowly. Jesse says, "Go get the bulldog!" I try to quietly wake the bulldog, but he snores as loud as the pregnant mare, and I end up shaking him. Franklin, the bulldog, protector of our home, finally wakes up. He sputters and snorts and plods to the basement door with me. Jesse says, "Get 'em Franklin." Franklin still half asleep, but now thinking there could be some excitement, starts forward, loses his balance, and falls like a sack of rocks down the stairs. Jesse and I are at first concerned, but then start laughing, as our surprise attack has now been blown. We go down after the "graceful" bulldog to search for the intruder.

Except for a scare from a Halloween dummy propped up in a corner that I had made last fall, the basement is clear. The kids must have left the lights on, and I don't know what could have caused the noise. Jesse suddenly looks at me and says, "Terry, go out to the barn, I can't explain it, but I believe that mare is foaling right now."

I tear out to the barn and flip on the lights. All the horses are looking toward the foaling stall across the aisle. I walk over to it, my heart pounding, look through the bars and see a little face with a white blaze looking at me from the straw. Missy is looking at me as though to say, *See what I made?* She is proud and protective but allows family members to handle the foal from head to toe.

We name him Jesters' Show Me The Money. His barn name is Comet. The Halle-Bopp Comet was over the barn in the weeks preceding his birth. I feel like a new mom myself and inspect Comet daily. I send out birth announcements with photos and drag everyone who comes over to the barn to see him. I ask Jesse if he would like to go out to the barn and look at our foal one more time. He looks at me and says, "Why? Has he changed in the last forty-five minutes?" I buy a four-roll pack of film and use it all up in three weeks.

My daughter, Jade, starts a baby book for him. Every time someone compliments me on the foal, I ask them, "Are you sure you like him? You're not just saying that, are you?" Dennis Lanham, the horse dentist, says, "Terry, of course I mean it. If a horse person gives you a compliment, shut up and accept it. If they don't like him, they won't say anything."

Comet is now two months old. He will let me groom him, pick up all four feet, lead him around, and I recently clipped his bridle path for the first time. Every time I hear him slurping his milk while he eats or see him playing and cavorting in the pasture I think how lucky I am to be living my dream.

Mindy, another of our broodmares, has also now been bred, and the container came via Federal Express, so I didn't have any embarrassing moments. Her ultrasound photo is on the wall under Comet's. She is due in late February or early March, depending upon how fickle she chooses to be.

I think I am a lot more professional and capable now. I feel calmer and wiser. The other day, I called my friend Will, who has been raising horses for years. I asked if I should be doing something to make my colt a better horse. "Sit on your hands," he told me. So now I am stockpiling 35-mm film.

My life is entirely run by a few four-leggeds who like me but would probably just as soon spend their time with the grass in the field. I, and others like me, have devoted my entire life to educating people about this magnificent creature. I wonder, how did I, GaWaNi Pony Boy, allow myself to be wooed into becoming a mouthpiece for these wise teachers? What spell did they use to lure me into the trap of being one of their spokespersons? I don't ever remember making a conscious decision to tour the world, teaching others about horse behavior. I don't ever remember saying, I shall muck stalls every day of my life, for the rest of my live-long days. And this fact, the fact that I never made the conscious decision to have my life run by horses, puts me at odds with my understanding of the universe. Think about the term "beast of burden." Sure, horses spent many years carrying the weight of many civilizations, but look who is now carrying the weight of the beast.

We feed horses only the finest grains twice daily. We make sure that they always have fresh, clean water. We bathe them, brush their hair, comb their manes, and massage their sore muscles. We constantly are buying them new shoes. Should they get cold, we drape winter coats over their backs. If it's not too cold, we comfort them with only a sheet. They see the dentist two to three times a year. We buy for them only the gentlest shampoos and exotic conditioners containing ingredients that most of us have never heard of. For no reason at all, they get treats at all times of the day and night. Are these offerings made to appease the king? We have been fooled! A huge segment of the human population has been deceived by what many have called a stupid animal. Horses lead us around by the nose and get us to do whatever they want us to do. They have manipulated and rearranged our way of life in such a way that our service to them is all that matters to us.

This creature is not so innocent. Given the opportunity, the horse will provoke from you an invitation into your life. It will then increase its demands on you until those demands are beyond your means. When your monetary resources are at their limit, you will be convinced that you have to purchase another horse, and then another and another. You will gradually begin to take on a weary appearance. You will begin to ignore normal societal pressures and concentrate on more basic needs such as food and sleep. Your life, although complex, will slowly become simpler. Patience, something we humans hate to succumb to, will become a natural tendency rather than an unattainable virtue. The clarity that comes from hard work will begin to show itself to you and the fog that permeates "life in the fast lane" will begin to lift. Then, as the fog lifts, you will begin to understand why so many have given in to the will of their masters—the horse.

Horses have been given the gift of a simple life. When we are willing to carry only a small portion of the weight that they have carried for centuries, horses bestow upon us the gift of simplicity. Is there any more cherished state in today's society than the bliss that exists in the uncomplicated? I thank the horses who have given clarity to many in a foggy world.

HORSES THROUGH THE EYES OF THE HEART AND THE LENS

by Gabrielle Boiselle

Early in the First World War, when I was four years old, soldiers were billeted on us and their horses turned out in the park. My nanny tells me that I perpetually escaped from her watchful eye, and was often to be found surrounded by enormous horses eating tidbits of grass that I picked for them after I had squeezed myself between the railings of the park to be among them. But one day when they missed me I was found sitting on the back of the pony that was kept for the governess cart. I was vainly trying to put its collar over its head by edging myself up its neck as I held the collar….From that day stable doors had to be locked against me, for I used to sit between the legs of enormous cart horses…and that, to my nurse, looked far too dangerous.

—from *I Should have Been Born in a Stable*
by Barbara Woodhouse

When I return from one

of my photo shoots, which can keep me away from home for several weeks, I go first to the stables to see my horses, even if it is the middle of the night. The feeling of their nostrils on my ears and the push from their heads as if to say, *Where have you been so long?* gives me the feeling of having come home. All the tension that was built up in my efforts to get the best and the most expressive pictures of horses slowly slips away and I feel suddenly exhausted. Getting back into the saddle for a long and wonderful ride into the forest on my stallion, with the dogs alongside, brings total relief. It is a kind of happiness, a special feeling of flying and total fulfillment, which, I am sure, I share with thousands of other women in the world.

My horses are a special kind of medicine for me that no doctor will ever be able to prescribe. They cure my frustration and depression; they have helped me through a lot of difficult situations. They share my happiness, too, and I have spent with them some of the most beautiful moments in my life. If there are decisions to be made or problems to be solved, I often sit in the stable on a pile of hay listening to the crunching noises of the horses eating their hay. The moon shines through the open stable door and the horses are transformed into big shadows. From time to time, some equine lips reach out to touch my hair, assuring me in the horse's way that everything is okay. In this peaceful atmosphere, I come to conclusions, and I see things I do not recognize during the day when I am busy in the office. My horses give me inspiration and comfort in being part of their lives. I belong to their hearts. Their acceptance and affection means very much to me.

I own eleven horses who I bred myself, now in the third generation. They were born in my stable and they will never leave until they move to another world. They are my guards and my angels. I feel their protection, and, bound together with all the other creatures, I think we are spiritually linked to each other.

As long as I can remember, horses have been my big love. This did not come by chance; it was meant to happen. I inherited this special "horse link" from my grandfather, who was known as a fine horseman. People came to see him and seek his advice if they could no longer get along with their horses. If he couldn't deal with these horses, their next stop would be the slaughterhouse. Grandma told me one story about him that shows extremely well his instincts about horses.

Grandpa took a little rest every day after lunch. The room where he rested was on an upper floor and faced the street. One summer day, as he lay with the window open, there came a coach thundering down the street. Even asleep Grandpa knew that something was wrong by the noise of the hooves on the pavement. He awoke and jumped out of the window in his socks. He ran beside the team of four horses, swung himself on the back of one of them, and brought them to a halt. The helpless driver had been totally out of control, but Grandpa knew immediately how to solve the problem.

My grandfather was a quiet man, I'm told. I never met him because he died before I was born. But he has passed over to me his special relationship with horses. It was quite apparent when I was very young that horses were meant to be my destiny. Everything started with a black Thoroughbred mare named Anouschka. In the life of everyone connected to horses there is one individual who has a certain meaning and who touches your feelings deeply. And there is always one horse who leads your desire and dreams in certain directions.

In my life it was this mare, Anouschka. She was an English Thoroughbred mare, jet-black, with

the kindest eyes in the world. One time when no one was looking, I crawled quickly on all fours over the yard toward the stable and into Anouschka's loose box. Quiet as a dormouse, I sat directly under the mare in the fresh-smelling straw. Anouschka did not make a single movement. The only sounds were the flicking of her tail and the soothing noise of chewing as she munched the hay. From time to time, her large, soft muzzle dropped toward me to sniff, then nudge me lightly and tenderly. I fell asleep in a state of total contentment. Anouschka was my house—her four legs formed the pillars and her belly was the roof. There, in my Anouschka house, I felt secure.

Outside in the yard, my family began to search for me. My shaggy canine playmate, Blacky, traced me to the stable. Whimpering with joy, Blacky betrayed me to the adults.

Anouschka was the best child-minder in the world. Her legs formed the support for my first attempts at walking, and later, on her back, I first knew the enthralling feeling of the freedom that is riding. Anouschka's rider placed me in front of her on the saddle as a copilot and we galloped along the banks of the Rhine. We overtook the ships sailing upstream and the wind brought tears to my eyes. I shouted and cheered. It was the most beautiful experience of my childhood.

Oh, that ride! That first ride!—most truly it was an epoch of my existence;
and I still look back to it with feeling of longing and regret.
People may talk of their first love—it is a very agreeable event, I dare say—
but give me the flush, and triumph and glorious sweat of a first ride, like mine of the mighty cob…

—George Borrow (from "Lavengro")

Horses mean a lot to me, but I do not want to create the impression that I am not able to communicate with people or that I have a strange social life. I have a lot of friends and a lot of affection in my life. I have had wonderful relationships and have experienced love in satisfying and beautiful ways. But the constant love in my life is my animals, especially the horses.

A lot of people ask me which horses I like most. They are not satisfied with my answer most of the time, but I really have no breed preferences. The kind of pictures I take shows that the special creature just then in front of my camera is the one I love most. Within each horse I see all other horses, and I try to visualize their grace and beauty. And at that moment I do not care if the subject is a famous, valuable Arabian stallion or a grade horse. I love all of them and I have learned on my travels around the world not to value a horse by its conformation and first appearance. It is nice to ride a good-looking horse, but when you have to cross dangerous mountains or stiff and slippery hills (as I did one time in Turkey), the ugly domestic ponies are adorable doing their job.

I love all horses, old and young, beautiful and ugly. It pains and disturbs me to see so-called nasty horses. They are just mistreated; no horse is a born killer. But I have, as well, met horses who can hardly be domesticated, who stay wild in their souls. They need to be turned loose and never ever be touched. This is the rule that we humans do not follow because we cannot accept not being the ones in control.

I thank God from the bottom of my heart to have received this wonderful gift of being a photographer, and to combine it with my love for horses, to express and to show their beauty. I know these pictures are touching the hearts of people and opening up their minds. Sometimes I can see it in the eyes of the person viewing my work. The beauty and grace of the horse trickles like small drops of water into the person's soul, watering the thirsty plant of emotions inside. I do not see it as my achievement. I am just the "in between."

A lot of people cannot see their own horses with my eyes. It happens quite often when clients are looking at the images after the photo shoots. They hardly recognize their own horses, and spontaneously tell me that they never had a clue about this side or that expression. Being with the horses all day shuts down their capacity of seeing. I have experienced this many times. I guess I can look behind the reality to see just a bit more.

It is fun sometimes to figure out why a certain person has a certain horse. Sometimes, they do not seem to fit with each other in conformation or temper. But I learned a long time ago that people instinctively select horses for their inner needs. Or it could happen, as well, that a horse picks his new owner. Even people who have already decided to buy another horse end up with special, difficult, or mistreated horses, instead of the easy-going ones they had their minds set on. Horses are meant to be medicine for the humans. They give us lessons that we need in life and it doesn't matter if we are children or adults. We get what we need.

I am one of the very lucky people for whom horses are not only a personal hobby but a profession as well. Only a few can say that their lives are the fulfillment of their dreams. I can combine the things I love most in my private and professional lives, to live with and through and for horses, to act as a photographer and as an artist, to travel to the most beautiful places in the world, and to meet inspiring people from all social levels. All this costs, on the other hand, a lot of energy and effort to hold up my spiritual alertness and the willingness to learn a new lesson from life every day—to keep growing. We all know that what we do is more than a job. It is a challenge. And as in the lives of other people, there are a lot of setbacks in mine too. The film developing goes wrong, clients don't or can't pay their bills, etc. But these obstacles cannot drag me down. There are always solutions. Life offers too many wonderful gifts for me to be concerned about the daily difficulties.

Every day there are so many wonders to discover and so many gifts along the way. You need only to see them. The small and quiet moments are the most fulfilling ones. Sitting outside in the midst of flowers and the smell of green grass, watching a foal discovering the world with its eyes—this is the most wonderful reward one could receive.

I look further. There is the horizon. There is the light. There is my way. I am following the tracks of the horses.

Gabrielle mentions in her essay that she "loves all horses, beautiful and ugly" and that "it pains and disturbs her to see so-called nasty horses." I have met quite a few horses who were introduced to me, by their owners, as nasty, mean, mean-spirited, ornery, incorrigible, psycho, and the list goes on. Horses, with very few exceptions, cannot be any of these things. They cannot be these things because it is not in their nature to be them. With the extremely rare exception, it is simply impossible for a horse to behave outside of the boundaries that his nature provides. The exception, of course, is any animal who is afflicted with any number of psychological disorders.

I have heard many trainers, especially the well-known ones, say that there are no bad horses; only bad trainers. I do not agree. Just as with humans and any other high-functioning animal, diseases and disorders can do horrible things to the brain. Just as we can suffer psychoses, so can horses. I'm not explaining this exception to be used as a disclaimer of any sort or to infer that any difficulties you may be experiencing might simply be psychological disorders. The cases are rare, but they do exist, and the diagnosis is fairly simple. Because horses operate so strictly within their nature, when we see one acting outside of that nature, we might start to look for a physical problem having to do with brain function. In other words, if your horse sleeps on his back with his legs in the air and spits like a camel and is in the habit of eating small dogs, you may very well be dealing with a psychological problem.

For the other 99.9 percent of us, we are probably misinterpreting behaviors or communications. Horses cannot be mean! What is a mean horse? One that steals hay from another? This is opportunistic behavior and if horses are anything, they are opportunistic. Is a horse who bites and kicks mean? All horses bite and kick, but they never do it to members of the herd that are of higher status than themselves. Is a mean spirited horse some sort of Satan horse who wishes, deep down, to see the demise of all other creatures? Incorrigible is a word usually used by teachers who do not possess enough patience to get the job done.

Of course we use most of these negatives out of our own frustration, but it is important to think about their meanings. Any time we refer to a horse as mean, we are anthropomorphizing the horse. If we continue to think of the horse as something that it is not, this thinking will slowly creep into all areas of our training and before we know it, we will be treating our horses like dogs and teenagers.

If we think of a horse as being mean, we respond to the horse in the same way that we respond to mean people. Some of us will be afraid, some of us will be ready to fight, and others will avoid the situation completely. Horses who have owners in the last category will either spend the rest of their lives in a pasture without having to deal with humans or be taken to the sale barn. If we think of a "mean" horse properly, we will see clearly that the horse is not mean, but, rather, aggressive.

Within the horse's definition of aggressive, *there is no anger. Aggression is simply a natural way for horses to improve their standard of living. Aggression allows a horse to test the waters in the* herd. If aggression is met with submission, then the horse has moved up one notch in the herd. If aggression is met with dominance, then nothing changes. If your "mean" horse challenges you and you do not meet the challenge with matching or exceeding aggression, your standard of living (in herd language) goes down and your horse's goes up.

I've met, had conversations with, and developed relationships with thousands of horses. I have met only two mean horses. One of these mean horses was diagnosed with a blood sugar imbalance and after being treated with medication was no longer mean. The other went undiagnosed and is in a Tennessee pasture living out his days without having to be bothered by any nasty humans. He's been there for sixteen years now.

KINDNESS, PATIENCE, FRIENDSHIP, AND TIME FOR PLAY

by Frankie Chesler

There is no secret so close
as that between a rider
and his horse.

—Robert Smith Surtees

Since before there were written words, people—especially women—have had a mystical relationship with horses. I believe that women encourage horses to listen, while men have a tendency to demand that horses listen. The finesse that most female riders have with horses can be attributed to the lack of upper body strength. Women are forced to seek out more creative ways to communicate with their horses.

The vocabulary of silent language permits women to communicate naturally with horses. Women tend to be more nurturing than men, and I think a woman's patience, understanding, and unconditional love helps her empathize with horses. With patience, a respect forms between horse and woman, and permits them to act and ride and be as one. Working with and riding horses is a lot like dancing. Those who can be gentle and fluid tend to be the best.

I believe that most warm-blooded animals react favorably to kindness. With kindness, I have developed a closeness with horses. Horses have allowed me to get close enough to them that we have been able sense what the other was thinking. I have always had more success with horses who have allowed me to become their friends, even their best friends.

I have learned so much about my horses just by having fun with them. Some of the horses swim with me. I hold onto their tails and they pull me up out of the pond. I often go in-line skating with my horses. I have a lead rope in one hand and a horse's tail in the other, and he or she pulls me up and down the driveway. Recently, I fashioned a wheelbarrow into a driving cart. The horses are amazingly tolerant of my homemade contraption. My veterinarian was so impressed by its construction that he asked to have his own turn on it. I believe that the time spent playing with and having fun with my horses is what really cements the bond between us.

One of the things that I really enjoy about Frankie is the importance that she places on playing with her horse. Play, in its purest form, is good for horses and good for humans. If you have been to one of my seminars, though, you may be saying to yourself, But, Pony, you told me that games are counterproductive to the relationship between horse and trainer. Games, in my opinion, are a good way to simplify concepts and to put those concepts into action, but they can also be counterproductive to the horse-human relationship; but play is good.

Last summer I vacationed for two weeks at the beach, and I played. I stood in the water where the waves were breaking and got slammed in the back and dragged up the beach. Now that was fun, but it was not a game. I also sat in a beach chair and dug a trench as deep as I could with my foot for an hour and a half. Again, really fun, but not a game.

So why am I such a party pooper when it comes to playing games with horses? Because to horses, games are not fun. Very few games were designed for pure enjoyment. Games sharpen skills, bolster memories, provide associations in the brain, promote fellowship, boost morale, exercise muscles, etc. Whereas play is pure and simple fun, very few games were designed with the sole objective of having fun. Fun to a horse is picking up a water bucket and letting it drop over and over again. Fun to a horse is trotting around a pasture, head and tail high, until something else is more fun. Fun to a horse is grass, and lots of it.

So, if you and your horse enjoy taking walks together, have fun! If you and your horse like to lie in the warm afternoon sun, have fun! But if you really enjoy playing the game of run around the cones, think again about how much fun your horse is having. When you are finished sharpening skills, exercising muscles, strengthening memories, and learning—go have fun with your horse.

AN INTUITIVE EDGE

by Mary Midkiff

An extra pressure,
a silent rebuke,
an unseen praising,
a firm correction:
all these passed between us
as through telegraph wires.

—Christilot Hanson Boylen

There is a natural affinity between women and horses. Women relate to horses on many levels and in so many ways. Trying to unlock every aspect of this magical partnership takes a lifetime of discovery. Here are a few thoughts on our partnership with horses derived from my book, _Fitness, Performance, and the Female Equestrian_.

There is a special bond between women and horses, something so basic it creates an immediate foundation for a relationship and a launching pad for most everything we want to do with a horse. We're passionate about horses; they sense it. We have a natural advantage in working with them, not unlike the bond between mother and child, that operates through good times and bad, through complicated tasks and easy ones.

Women are gatherers, nurtures, and teachers while men are proficient at spatial tasks, hunting, and defense. Through history, women have spent most of our time teaching and caring for the young. We have an innate ability to read emotions learned first by reading babies' cues without language. It all adds up to a woman's "intuition," not the abstract concept typically referenced in wonder by men but rather a very real ability to understand and predict based on behavior. Most of us have it, even if we haven't consciously used it or have allowed it to slip into disuse.

These female traits carry into the horse world and translate into positive behaviors and messages that can allow the horse to be more relaxed and more trusting, and ultimately perform to its potential, in partnership with the human female. After all, a relationship with horses is one of our most cherished, and they feel it through the positive and loving energy coming from us.

Think about it. What kind of person would work best with horses' behavioral characteristics? Chances are, you've begun to think in terms of the gentle touch, a soft but firm voice, an intuitive sense for the factors triggering a behavior, a calming effect, sensitivity instead of force, finesse over power, cooperation over dominance, and a constant search for more meaningful communication. This description certainly fits the human female. Women want to tame, save, and nurture the beast.

Recreational horse activities and sport riding are now largely dominated by young and adult women. From backyard horse keeping and training through Olympic level and top rodeo competition, women have become the predominant participants

and the key economic force. If you think about it, there is good reason for this.

Equestrian activities collectively represent one of the very few sports in which women compete on equal terms with men. The horse is the equalizer. The horse compensates for the inherent disparities in strength between men and women, and puts the "game" on a different field. That field promotes qualities and traits in which women can excel, such as finesse, touch, and understanding. This in no way disparages the competitiveness of women. Properly channeled, these capabilities translate into tremendous athletic performance by the horse/rider team (rather than the individual). And team performance is, after all, the essence of great riding.

While discussing her views on women and horses,
Mary Midkiff says, "We are passionate about horses; they sense it." How do they
sense it? For years I've danced around the subject of whether and how horses
sense things. The acronym ESP has become almost taboo in our society. Mind
reading, ESP, psychic—these are labels that we have put on abilities that most liv-
ing creatures on earth posses. But how do we explain this natural phenomenon without
delving into what is now called the paranormal?

Any female rider—or half-awake male rider—knows that there is more to the horse's mind
than just physical cues and rote memory. In Horse, Follow Closely, *I called this ability focal com-*
munication because I believe it best describes the phenomenon. Horses know what you are focusing
on. Not necessarily what you are visually focusing on, but rather what your mind is focusing on.

The most obvious example of focal communication can be witnessed when watching any group
of animals that is designed to move or act as one entity. In a herd or a school or a flock, it is imper-
ative that everyone works as a unit. The purpose of any of these groups is to ensure the safety of all
individuals by providing a large, confusing target and by intimidating the predator with the sheer
size of the group. Fish have been given a special organ, the lateral line, that enables them to physi-
cally feel what other members are doing. For herds and flocks, the feel is more refined.

In a herd, there is a leader and many followers. If the herd is put into a fleeing situation, it is
imperative that every member knows what is going on in the mind of the leader. Our first inclina-
tion is to deduce that if herd animals simply watch the herd member in front of them, the herd will
move in the same general direction. But taking cues visually would create a serpentine pattern
among the fleeing herd. A slight delay in response time between members would mean that if the
leader moved left, the last in line would also move left but his actions would be delayed. Herds do not
move in a serpentine pattern. Every member of the herd moves in the same direction simultaneous-
ly. By focusing on the whole of the herd, not on the individuals that it is made of, horses can antic-
ipate the movements of the leader. To begin to understand this we must think of the herd as a single
organism held together by the collective consciousness of its members.

So what does this mean to us, the human leader of the two-member herd? This means that we can
communicate most of our intentions by simply focusing on an action. Horses possess the ability to read
our focus, and if we ignore this ability our horses become numb to our requests. Enter equine boredom
and some behavioral problems. I've never met a high-level jumper who became bored on course. I've also
never met a high-level jumper rider who had the time to let his or her focus wander from the task at hand.
When a horse balks at a jump, what I usually hear from the rider later is, I wasn't focused *or* I wasn't con-
centrating or I lost my focus, *not* I didn't spur him enough *or* He didn't interpret my leg properly.

What about body language? Do women speak a different kind of body language than men do? I do
not think that men speak a different body language than women do, but I do think that men and women

talk about different things with their bodies. A lot of people are on the equine body language kick. I often hear body language referred to as if this new language has been discovered in some deep dark cave in Tibet. You do not have a choice but to speak with your physical expressions. It is not something you begin doing because a trainer shows you what to do. It is something you do all the time. We can try to mask our body language, but usually all this says is I'm guarded, stay away, *or* I'm trying to hide something. *If I had to teach people how to speak human body language, I would tell them to do everything they have always done and don't think about the messages that their bodies are conveying.*

Horses are expert body language readers. They are not terribly vocal creatures, and thus rely on the more honest language of physical expression. Body language is quite easy. Devote your focus to an idea or action and your body will do the rest.

Too often, my horses have been able to uncover my best efforts at masking my body language. If my horses are at pasture and I approach the gate, they will, without fail, come galloping to the gate to greet me. Because I have established myself as alpha of the herd, they report to the leader and wait for their orders. Sometimes, I am late and need to catch one of the horses to take with me. I begin to think about, or focus on, the act of catching the horse. After I realize that I am focusing on catching the horse, a predatory action, I remember that he can read my body language and will likely run away from me. I must not focus on catching him. To better understand my horses, I have even approached the pasture attempting to look like I was going to catch them and every time they came bounding up to say hello. Our body language does not lie. Our body language is determined by what we are focusing on. Horses can decipher that which we are focusing on and if we remember this, we can communicate better with our horses.

As for the differences in what men and women focus on when in the presence of horses; if women naturally focus on the horse's feelings and mood, on nurturing, calmness, cooperation, and teaching, then horses will become more inclined to bond, respond, cooperate, be nurtured, and enjoy their company. If men naturally focus on force, power, tasks, and dominance, then the horse will interpret this focus appropriately.

85

A CONVERSATION WITH HELEN KITNER CRABTREE

by GaWaNi Pony Boy

A good horse
makes short miles.

—George Elliot

I called Mrs. Crabtree for the first time on a summer evening in 1999. I asked her why she thought women and girls are attracted universally to horses.

"Well, to be perfectly honest with you I have no earthly idea," she answered.

In a matter of twelve words, Mrs. Crabtree was able to stop my questioning, shoot down my preconceptions of her or her answer, and take complete control of the conversation. In reflection, it is not surprising that this great trainer was able to control the direction of things so neatly. I now became the student.

"I was a professional at eleven," she began. "Now, this was during the Depression, and there were many men feeding their whole families on a dollar a day. I got paid a dollar a day for training horses—something I gladly would have done for much less money.

"I know it's a little ridiculous when somebody claims to have been a professional at age eleven, but actually, by definition, I was. People came to me. I didn't go to them. They found out about the crazy Kitner girl who could ride horses, and these old-time farmers would just bring 'em in.

"I didn't get into the equitation until much later, because at the time, I didn't even know there was such a word. I might have known there was such a thing as horsemanship, and I showed all these horses and ponies and everything that I had around. It wasn't that I was setting out to show something or train something, it was the condition in which these horses came in. I'll tell you, most of them were a little dangerous as far as some strangers thought, which made it interesting—very interesting—to me. But my parents understood me enough to trust me and my judgement.

"But most of the horses I got were what we called spoiled horses. I know what you do in your clinics and I know that you know exactly what I'm talking about when I say spoiled horses. Farmers would call up and ask if I would take their horse and I'd say, 'Well how far along is she?' and they'd say 'Ooh, she's fine, I ride her every day.' Well that can translate into 'She bucked me off yesterday and nearly broke my butt.' Some of the horses were okay, some of them would run off, but most people were there to see me because they couldn't handle their horses.

"I remember one particular horse who I had to teach not to run off. My dad said that I damn near killed her, but she didn't run off after that. You know I learned by doing, like so many people do. But God gave me a lot of talent when it came to working with horses. I can't brag on that. It's what you do with that talent, if you're willing to work (and God knows I'm a workaholic) that matters. And people who are successful have to be workaholics; if they are not, they're not gonna make it.

"You can't be on and off about—and this is not a pun either—your horse training. It's an everyday thing, and you have to be satisfied with a tiny little bit of progress. If a horse is one millimeter better than he was when you got on him then you've done a good job. You've got to aim for that each day without aiming for too much, and you've got to be smart enough to know when that horse is improving. And some people don't! If he takes one or two good steps, they think, 'Oh my goodness he's ready for the five-gaited stakes at Louisville.' You have to be smart enough to recognize the tiny little efforts that the horse is making as you go along.

"You don't do anything on a horse that doesn't have some effect, one way or the other. When things fall apart, one of two things has happened. Either you set out to do something positive and failed at it, or you set out to do one thing and told the horse something else and then you wonder what went wrong. Sure it's physical, but that's not all of it. Heck, I was once a top-seeded tennis player and that was fine but it didn't do a thing for my brain as far as horses were concerned. That came from God.

"You can't just look at where the head and neck go, and whether he bends to your leg the way you want him to. You have to look at the big picture. Is he capable of what you're asking, and are you capable of teaching it? If you're patient enough and stay with it day after day after day and can be satisfied with tiny results, then you and the horse will be happy."

Helen and her husband ran a public stable ("always have"), and they hired people to do the grooming. She spent many hours training these people who took care of these horses so that they didn't undo anything that she had done.

"We would spend at least an hour a day with each and every horse, whether it be on the ground or under saddle," she says fondly. "We worked those horses every day. One day, a horse would need to be driven and another day, he would be on long lines, and another day he wanted to be ridden." Then she adds, "Oh. . . I miss this so much!"

I asked her which part she misses the most.

"I rode in my last show when I was seventy-five. I'd be doing it right now but with macular degeneration and everything else I just can't do the things I used to.

"A couple of weeks ago, at the Kentucky State Fair—our world's championship—I was given the Audrie Guthrie award for a lifetime of helping the horse business. I've gotten other awards, Judge Emeritus, an honorary doctorate, I mean you go through them and, well, I was the first woman to be named Horse Trainer of the Year and a lot of people don't understand. It's been a struggle, you know?

"I remember once judging Morgan horses up in Albany. A fellow up there whose father I knew because I had shown with him, just couldn't seem to get beyond second or third place. It was just the kind of horses he had. And as a judge, if you're wide-awake, you know it's not up to you to help riders. You just judge what you see. This young man wanted to meet with me after the show and I knew it was a complaint. His father was there, too, with his two boys. The young fellow said to me, 'You know, you just can't seem to tie me better than second or third.' I said, 'I'm not here to help you or hinder you. I'm here to judge what I see.' And he said, 'Well, you's prejudice.' He was a black fellow, and when he had the nerve to say that to me I hit the ceiling.

"'Prejudiced?' I repeated. 'I could give you lessons on prejudice! Do you think I didn't fight prejudice all the way up the ladder? Do you think that all those old-time horse trainers—every one of them a man—didn't give me my share of prejudice? Don't give me that bunk!

"I had to fight plenty of prejudice when I was coming up, but do you know how I did it?"

I couldn't wait. "How?"

"I smiled at everybody and beat the hell out of them! I liked everybody, but then I tended to my knitting and they had to deal with it."

Mrs. Crabtree has put up with a lot and has laid the groundwork for those who followed. I wondered at what point this remarkable woman had coped with the most harassment from other riders or trainers about being a woman. She said it was her teenage years, when she was competing and trying to get into the championships and open classes.

"Back then, they didn't have all these amateur classes. They didn't have equitation classes. You just showed against the best there was. Most people were nice to me because I was nice to them. And the reason I was nice to them was because they were my idols. I tried not to be a pest, but I think the nicest thing that you can do is to go around to someone you respect and ask for advice. I was not above that. Most of them would help me, and I soon got them all on my side. They all wanted to help me because I asked for their help. But lots of times, you would hear a comment from the stands, like, 'What in the world is that girl doing out there with all those men?' and I always just nodded to them. Prejudice is a very poor excuse for inadequacy.

"You know, the last little horse that I broke was when I was seventy-five. You'd think after all those years there would be nothing left to learn. But this horse pointed something out to me. I'm a great believer in body weight and letting a horse respond to your balance. I had developed a habit over all these years of switching the bight of the reins over to the outside because these were show animals and the whole picture was neater with the bight of the reins on the side not facing the judge. I would pitch the reins over and use a leg aid to turn the horse, and barely feather his mouth, if that. One day, I flipped the reins over and he turned right around on me. I thought, *Good heavens!* You know I didn't realize the extent to which I had been teaching this horse. I knew my own logic for it, but I didn't know the point to which it soaked in. He was a wonderful horse. He got to the point where I could get him to change leads on every other stride just by flipping those reins.

"But he enjoyed work. He was never ornery, and I never took a whip to him, or yanked or jerked him. I'm not above knocking a horse down to his knees if he needs it, but that is usually not necessary. If you run into one of those, you get rid of him as soon as you can. You've got to enjoy every moment on a horse's back and there has to be a reason for what you're doing. And you can't make up your own reasons. If you did, you could just buy a sawhorse and a rope and save yourself a lot of money. This horse thing won't ever turn you loose."

Evidently not. And what a joy to know that. Before I left, Mrs. Crabtree told me a touching story, which I'd like to share with you just as she told it to me.

"Back when I won the Medal Class, there was a young man who came to me from up East. I had seen him at the New York show. I saw him and his horse. He had a mare whose head you couldn't set with a crowbar. But he never did anything wrong. He came down and moved the mare in with us.

"Now you talk about prejudice. In equitation the judges wouldn't take a boy seriously. I would see Eddie go in the ring and do a beautiful job and I would see the judges look and then when they saw he was a boy, their eyes would just hop right over him to the next rider. I thought, *How long is he going to put up with this?* His mare

kept getting better and better. One day, he was showing at Louisville in the championship, and it looked like he was an easy winner. He ended up fifth or sixth.

"Do you know what he said to me when he came out of the ring? He said, 'Mrs. Crabtree, I believe I got that mare's head set better today then I ever have.' I wanted to hug him!

"He stayed out of the Korean War, but he was in an automobile accident. He broke his back and was paralyzed from the waist down. I called to talk to him on the phone many a time and urged him to be an instructor because he would make such a great one. Finally, he called me from Florida and said he was on his way. 'I'm gonna come up and get with my old trainer to do some instructing and I want to come up to Simpsonville to see you and Mr. Crabtree.' I said, 'Eddie, you be careful crossing those mountains.' He had one of those vans that's controlled by hand levers.

"The next day, I had this urge to get home. I hadn't been home five minutes when the phone rang. A voice said, 'This is Eddie's aunt and he was coming to visit you.' I said, 'What do you mean, was?' She said 'His van went off of the mountain last night and killed him.'

"But what an inspiration he was to everybody—a good-looking young man who was just as nice to the eight year olds as he was to the seventeen year olds, and all he was worried about was that his mare's head was set right. He was in it for the right reasons. I think all these hours I've spent, working with these horses and riders, he made it worthwhile when he said that to me."

As I left, I thanked her for the education.

WATERCOLORS

by Sarah Lynn Richards

*The air of heaven
is that which blows between
a horse's ears.*

—Arabian Proverb

In my work as an artist and a therapist, I have been struck many times by the nature of human beings. We have been struggling since we first came to consciousness to understand ourselves as a people and as individuals. That which we call self—the essential heart or soul of one—is particularly elusive. It is often only through symbols and metaphor that we can catch glimpses of the true nature of self. In powerful and repetitive motifs, we explore and express what we are. Often, it seems, the clearest picture comes in reflected form.

We have been infatuated with horses for a long time. Their image has been burned onto cave walls, their form sculpted, painted. They have meant power, food, prestige. Perhaps like no other animal, they have lit hearts on fire with their spirit. The hearts of women in this age seem to be particularly afire in their relationship to *Equus*. At a time when women are beginning to realize their own unique potential, as they pull on the robes of powerful people, there are clues that challenging work is yet to be done. From the folds of these bright new clothes fly a few moths. Through our relationship to the horse we may be able to know a bit about ourselves and tug these new things into forms that accentuate our intrinsic abilities.

Through my own experiences as a woman, I have encountered both the powerful presence of an emerging female spirit and the hobbling malaise that still nips at its heels. I think that a great deal of the energy in my paintings comes from a nameless, pulsing feminine energy that I borrow but don't own. This energy is impossible to quantify, difficult to pin down with words. Yet, when women feel it—Her—leaping in their chests, taking flight in their hands, and directing them beyond reason, they recognize Her with a part of them that defies capture. In the work of therapy, we feel about in the dark for Her, call out Her name, and rejoice when we are reunited with this energy.

Maybe our relationship with the horse is part of this. We are drawn to this animal who is domesticated and tamed but who can never really be divorced from its wild instinctive nature. Maybe we recognize a common spirit with this wonderful creature, the horse.

There is a horse named Friday who lives on my family's farm. Saved from the knackers years ago, he is an old horse, too old to ride. He has lived in the same three-acre pasture for the better part of a dozen years and the ground inside the perimeter of the fence has been worn to a hardpan from his hooves as he makes his daily rounds of the field. At some point, we discovered the fence that had bordered the field had given way and lay in pieces on the ground. It had apparently been that way for a while.

It is a puzzle as to why Friday remained within the boundary when nothing prevented his escape to the lush grass on the other side. We suppose that Friday is of the mind that the barrier is still there, and each day walks past the gap as if the fence were intact. It is perplexing and a little humorous to watch him yearn for the green grass just on the other side of the "fence" when nothing keeps him from walking to it, nothing we can see. If one takes pity on the old horse, one can take a handful of forelock and lead him through the gap to the greenery on the other side. He hops and bucks in ecstasy at release on the far side, free at last.

As human beings, we, too, must make our choices, build our fences and remain safe or forsake safety for the riskier and more fulfilling life without them. It would be unfair to suggest that Friday has made a conscious choice about his life; it is only through a rather anthropomorphic peephole that we can observe and speculate on his state. If, however, we stop and look deeper, we may see some symbolic reflections into our own somewhat shadowy doings.

Although the fence is no longer standing, its functional existence has been maintained within Friday. Though these invisible barriers keep him tightly contained, they also keep him safe. Friday has been domesticated and has lost all sense of how to exist on his own. He has learned to be polite, not to kick, not to bite, and he eats and drinks from plastic buckets. Kicking and biting are natural defenses of wild horses, as are the ability to find food and water on their own. Without these skills, Friday is fairly helpless. He relies on fences to provide shelter from a threatening world, but he is also contained by them.

Does this resemble in any way the modern woman's struggle to exist? In her quest for safety, has she accepted the restrictions offered by her society? Don't bite, don't kick, eat this, drink this, look like this, walk like this, talk like this. Perfection equals protection? Has she internalized these complex familial and cultural standards and made them her own? If this is so, she has (unconsciously) struck a bargain. She will occupy only the space that is prescribed, she will take up less space than her natural or whole self would, but she

will be safe. It is a tradeoff, and may seem like a fair one if choices are few. It is, however, the very state of this safety that prevents wholeness and growth for the individual.

All around us, women are succeeding and changing the definition of female. And yet, we still seem to be out of balance. We seem to be straddling some fences between being modern women, living in a masculine society, and a deep true sense of connection to our feminine roots. But what do *masculine* and *feminine* mean—not the modern advertising messages, but the deeper, older meaning?

In nature, there are both feminine and masculine elements, yin and yang in Chinese culture. In nature, we see the masculine element in those things that embody doing: light, heat, dividing, and initiation. All that is defined and concrete. The feminine element is the world of being: intuition, creation, life, dark, and undifferentiated. These two elements balance and complement each other. When the natural way of things is respected, a balance will exist and things will seem easy. Our culture is planted in the masculine, the yang, the pursuit of control and mastery. The feminine, the yin—the art of being—has been feared and thrown out of the paddock. Maybe we feel safer without it, but we suffer from imbalance.

This imbalance is often manifested in women's relationship to their bodies. I feel it in women I know, I read about it in the literature, I overhear it in the checkout line at the grocery store. Many of us hate our bodies. We hate how fat they get, we hate that we have to feed them. An overwhelming number of us feel as if we are at war with our bodies.

If our femininity—our connection to a feminine element—is manifested in our bodies, then what is it saying about a culture so upset by robust female shapes? Maybe we are a bit like Friday ourselves. In a culture where being a large or voracious woman can bring subtle or outright scorn, we begin to see where our own fences lie.

We may use the woman with anorexia nervosa as an extreme example of what many women wished they looked like. If she is anything, the woman with anorexia is busy, compelled even to narrow and restrict, sometimes to the point of just existing and sometimes to nonliving. She rejects her appetites and instincts. The anorexic's body is a graphic vision of her tradeoff. She is the picture of control, of restricted femininity. In her compulsive controlling lies her safety, and ironically her restriction in a much more profound way. Caught up as she is in her rituals, she is unable to even feel her natural instincts, which in and of themselves are balanced and wholesome. Her fences, built from within and without, are her protective boundary and her prison.

Historically, both women and horses have had to divorce themselves from their more spirited and natural habits in order to live without harassment. We have both been taught to shape and carry our bodies just so, and what we cannot do alone, some sort of mechanical intervention can easily be arranged to forcibly bring it. In exchange for safety both women and horses have lost a wilder, more spirited side, a part of themselves that wholly embraces life, a part that embodies and encircles their potential. How joyless to live only within the boundaries of perfection.

Maybe our love and longing for horses has to

do with recognition and a shared path. We see in them exalted free spirits, instinctive and intuitive. We recognize the adaptations they have had to make, and we feel a secret communion. We, too, have a spirited and instinctive nature. And yet we live in a culture where instinct must defer to science, where communion must defer to hierarchy.

Most recently there have been breakthroughs in our thinking about horses and their training. We have begun to discover, actually rediscover, that they already have language, a natural way of relating and learning. We are amazed at what they can do. Suddenly, doors open and the once impossible becomes obvious. Women, too, have language and a way of relating, an instinctive and spirited way of being that has always existed.

When it is rediscovered, it is instantly recognized and welcomed. "Hah!" With a clap of hands and a knowing grin, we recognize our wild sisters.

It is the nature of things to yearn for wholeness. Wholeness is a wild (natural) and powerful element that is rhythmically inventive. Something that even in the visceral mess of birth is ingeniously creative and productive. It is something far removed from the sanitized, predictable, assembly-line production with which our society is so infatuated. The imbalance has come because something has been removed from the circle of self. Straight lines abound, but our energy is limited. Finding the pieces that have been removed from the circle is a unique task. Like the circle itself, it is work that is entirely simple and unbelievably complex at the same time.

It is hard to know what powerful women are like. The thread that used to link powerful women together has been dropped. This thread that bound many women and taught them rightful power is difficult to find, but powerful women still exist.

Powerful women are comfortable with their bodies. They are proud of their strength. These women are not ashamed of their wrinkles, not ashamed of gray hair or hearty laughter. It is part of their strength. They are not powerful over others, they are powerful within themselves. These women have lost battles of course, but they have done the work of reclamation and they are fed by the energy that comes from being whole.

As we begin to see the inherent wisdom of the earth, our bodies, and nature in general, we start to accept what first appeared to be wild and frightful as wholesome and instinctive. Our relationship with the horse can be seen as reflecting our relationship with nature and our own selves. We have been at once awestruck, frightened, controlling, and, more recently, horses' students. We see that instinctive, spirited energy has a place in their survival, and maybe our own as well.

We may become more balanced and whole if we as a culture could embrace variance in color, shape, and size. Rejecting the masculine, or yang, entirely would only produce a mirror opposite of our current imbalance. Both yin and yang together (masculine-feminine) create circle, balance, ecology, self, where all elements are represented and valued. Embracing a true feminine element, where creativity, connectedness, and nurturance flourishes would reunite two ends of a straight line to form one continuous whole.

THE HORSE IN THE WOMAN'S ROLE

by Lisa Kiser

Where in this wide world can man find nobility without pride,
friendship without envy, or beauty without vanity?
Here, where grace is laced with muscle,
and strength by gentleness confined.
He serves without servility, has fought without enmity.
There is nothing so powerful, nothing less violent;
nothing as quick, nothing more patient.
The world's past has been borne on his back.
We are his heirs; he is our inheritance.
The horse.

— Ronald Duncan in *Ode to the Horse*

Over the years, I have pondered the evident connection between women and horses. The numbers speak for themselves concerning the undeniable bond we share, but they don't answer one question: Why? I have my own theories on the bond between woman and horses, which I have cultivated as an armchair pursuit.

One of my theories is that women identify with horses. The horse is a visually appealing creature. Its large eyes, leggy stature, and flowing mane seem to give it a physical nature similar to how both men and women in many cultures view women. Beauty, softness, grace, delicacy; these are things we think of as feminine qualities. And, like women—for whom so much emphasis is placed on appearance—horses have endured the endless upkeep of having their manes braided; their nails polished; their whiskers trimmed; their hair shined, conditioned, and even colored; and their eyes accentuated with make-up. But beyond appearance, take a look at the other similarities between horses and the traditional roles of women.

Horses are creatures of work. They have been the engines of day-to-day life. They've been used for war, sport, hunting, transportation, farming, and, to a lesser extent, currency. All these activities have traditionally been the domain of men, but the roles that horses play in these activities— the roles of servant, trophy, commodity, and status symbol—are the same roles that women (to our modern-day chagrin) have played. The similarity is noticed also in an old saying, "The West was hard on women and horses."

Perhaps women identify with the horse's role in our culture, not just in the horse's roles in day-to-day life. Perhaps we identify with something more deeply personal—with horses' relationship to men, traditionally the decision-makers and leaders of the family unit. My generation is likely the last to have observed these sweeping cultural sex roles in our formative years. But when one thinks of how horses have been bred, worked, and mined in the past, one sees the horse being required to submit to the wishes of humans, much as women in the recent past and even today have felt required to submit to the wishes of men.

I don't want to anthropomorphize. To a horse, a leader is a leader and a societal role is a societal role, regardless of whether that leader and that society are human or equine. Nor do I patently condemn the traditional societal structures between men and women. On the contrary, I believe that traditional roles of provision, survival and defense, child-rearing, and housekeeping were efficient and effective in those societies, and continue to be the best choice for some men and women who happily choose them today. However, speaking as a human observing horses' interactions with humans and women's traditional interactions with men, I see some similarities. And maybe other women do, too.

The emotional nature of working with horses may also appeal to women. Although no set of characteristics can be uniformly applied to either sex, women do tend to exhibit traits such as patience and gentleness more often than do men, making us all think of these things as feminine characteristics, no matter in whom we observe them. Girls and women are more likely to romanticize the horse, to believe in the myth of *the horse that only I can ride*.

Boys are raised to be problem solvers, to believe that persistence will always produce results, to believe that they can conquer anything. They are given the gift of the self-focused approach to life. Girls are led to value relationships, to observe others' reactions and body language, to keep the peace, to be sympathetic, and to nurture. That other-focused mentality is ideally suited to working with horses, especially high-strung, sensitive horses. Does the delicate challenge of training and riding such horses open up realms for women that we find irresistible? I think so.

It's interesting to me that virtually all of the "natural horsemanship" gurus and pioneers, the resistance-free trainers, are men. Tom Dorrance, Ray Hunt, John Lyons, Richard Shrake, Monty Roberts, and others have achieved fame in the horse world and beyond by proclaiming a more gentle, nonconfrontational way of training. If this is the more natural approach for women, why aren't these top trainers at least half women? I believe it's because the top horse trainers have traditionally been men, and the emergence of the new thinking comes from that percentage of those

men who flout the traditional ways of their forefathers. The women who have been using these methods instinctively for years may have either thought themselves odd ducks in the horse world or thought that these methods were simply common sense. They may not have thought to go on the lecture circuit with their ideas. Whatever the reason, I keep wondering if the remarkable revelations that strike men who search for a kinder, gentler way to teach horses might be attributable to their ability to acknowledge their feminine nature.

Another source of the deep connection between women and horses could be the dichotomy of the horse, evident from every angle. This fascinates me. They are lovely, yet dangerous. They are delicate despite their size.

Men seem (to us women, anyway) to be rather linear. They are multifaceted, but those facets all seem to fit in a logical order. In other words, men make sense, even when we don't agree. But ask any man if women make sense. Women display divergent qualities seemingly at odds. We are fragile and resilient, soft and strong, tender and fierce, stubborn and compliant, consistent and fickle, demanding and accommodating, maddening and irresistible.

Horses' instincts for self-preservation are strong, yet they are exceedingly patient with our demands and eager to please us. We begin to see contradictory qualities that make us wonder at the complexity and simplicity of this creature who so captivates and challenges us.

The horse represents, to many, what we humans strive to be: the best of what we can be in our finest hour, with none of the gossip, brutality, pettiness, stinginess, and bigotry. Horses are not thinking creatures in the self-aware, philosophical sense. Ironically, their innocent, unselfconscious qualities of nobility, beauty, and strength effortlessly achieve what we humans drive ourselves with religion, vanity, and ambition to achieve: balance, peace, admiration, ability, and purpose.

Many women are drawn to equestrian pursuits because the horse is the great equalizer. This is another theory of mine. The things that separate men and women in the home and workplace are irrelevant in most riding activities. Riding takes technical skill, knowledge, timing, balance, coordination, nerve, athletic fitness, and control of mind and body—things that are present equally in able-bodied men and women. Issues such as strength, size, height, age, cultural advantage, and the prejudices of others either don't matter or can be overcome. Just ask successful international riders such as Margie Goldstein, Betsy Steiner, and Susie Hutchison—all petite women—if women are just as capable of driving a rig, giving a vaccination, and packing a hoof as men are. They can't strong-arm a horse. But if you think about it, a man can't either. In a pulling match, the strongest man is no match for your average pony. So the main physical difference is a nonissue, and the advantage in getting horses to perform in ways that the horses respond to best is clearly that of the woman, or any person who approaches the horse with the feminine qualities of empathy, patience, emotional generosity, sincerity, and sensitivity.

And, delightfully, it works both ways. Horses enjoy this great equalizer quality that they give to humans. Mares, geldings, and stallions provide equal athletic successes to their owners and riders. Many female riders must enjoy the fact that male and female horses run, jump, *piaffe*, cut cattle, and run barrels with equal aplomb. As far as athleticism goes, there are few instances in which it is an advantage to be either a mare, gelding, or stallion. And this great equalizer applies to other factors, not just sex. When a skilled rider and a talented horse have a well-earned lucky round, characteristics such as height, age, sexual orientation, financial security, and race move out of the moment.

The vast majority of girls go through a phase in which they are enamoured of horses. From vastly divergent backgrounds, socioeconomic situations, and geographic areas, girls through the ages have become drawn to horses. For many, the years that bring other interests and obsessions—boys, cars, school, other sports, and career—displace their interest in horses, but the connection, the allure, is always present. A few turn this fascination into a vocation or avocation, a hobby, or even a lifelong career. The rest are there, where most of us once were, in our dreams.

In those dreams, we charge over hedges on a perfect frosty morning at the hunt. We race down the last furlong in the come-from-behind win of the year. We stun the judges in a sequined satin jacket atop a glossy plump champion pleasure horse. We ride on the beach with abandon at sunrise, the salt wind brushing water from our eyes and into our hair. We become the only entry to clear a triple combination at the Olympics, winning a medal for our country. We are the horse, on some level—that sweet, grassy breath; the salty, earthy smell; the soft, inquisitive gaze; the wild, courageous heart; the light, powerful stride; the silky, flying mane.

We are the horse, to men and to our ourselves.

I have been called a kinder, gentler trainer by everyone from radio show hosts to horse show announcers to book reviewers. I agree with Lisa on the point that these "natural" horse trainers are perhaps more in touch with their feminine side, but I must take issue with the terms kind *and* gentle. *I have spent years saying that if we want to cultivate lasting, productive relationships with horses, we must work within the boundaries of what they understand. The horse does not understand* kinder *and the horse does not understand* gentler. *I will explain.*

Kind is a word that we use to describe someone who goes out of his way to help others, someone who takes pleasure in not being confrontational, but rather enjoys helping others to succeed. I have never witnessed an animal go out of his way to help others. I have certainly never seen a wild horse taking pleasure in helping another to succeed. An animal who is kind would be seen traveling around the forest doing good deeds for different species.

It's not that horses would not be kind if they knew how to, it's that kindness is a human behavior. When it comes to teaching horses, I would just as soon take any method revolving around human behavior and throw them out the window.

As for gentler, gentle is certainly not a word that I would use to describe the nature of the horse. Horses can be quite gentle when showing affection or when mutual grooming is taking place, but during the teaching and training portion of their lives—which is the part we are talking about—gentleness is not an accurate descriptor. When a horse teaches another that he is of lower rank, the action is like lightning. Lightning is not gentle. When a horse teaches another to move away from a group of mares, he resembles a freight train. Freight trains are not gentle.

Now, it may sound like I am advocating rough-and-tough horse training methods, but I am not. I am simply saying that if we wish to be successful in our efforts with horses, we must think like horses, act like horses, and do what horses do. Horses possess an ability that humans, for the most part, have not mastered, aggression without anger. They don't pull punches and they don't hold grudges. Humans have a tendency to get angry, which stirs up aggression. So many times I have seen a rider get nipped by his or her mount (a status-reinforcing behavior) and react by kicking, screaming, hitting, and cursing at the horse. Not only does this behavior cause fear in the horse, but it also seems ludicrous to the horse. This is not how horses behave. To teach the horse, we must behave like the horse. What horses do understand is herd mate vs. predator. If you act like a herd mate, you will be perceived as one by your horse. If you behave like a predator, your horse's reactions will reflect your behavior.

A kinder, gentler trainer describes to me someone who uses human methods and behavior models to train horses. Most of what I know about horses was taught to me by horses. And none of them ever taught me to be anything but a confident, trusted, herd mate.

MY LOVE FOR HORSES

by Martha Josey

. . . and God took a handful of southerly wind,
blew his breath over it and created the horse. . .

—Bedouin Legend

Horses were such a major

part of my parents' life, it seemed only natural they would want to share that same love with me. Daddy, holding me in his arms, took me for my first ride when I was just a few days old. I really believe that's where it all started, because my family said my first word was *horse*.

Daddy started his horse career with standardbreds, but soon turned his interest to quarter horses. He brought one of the first really good quarter horse stallions, named Thumper, to the east Texas area. Even though I was very young, Daddy's deep feeling for his horses became a part of me. I have fond memories of early rides on my first horse, a pony named Chigger, not much more than fifty inches tall. By age eight, I had already spent countless hours in the saddle, riding alongside Daddy, checking out our cows, cornfields, and hay crop. The rest of the family helped with our horse operation in many ways, but Daddy and I just couldn't get enough. Caring for our horses was our life.

I attended a local rodeo one weekend and it changed my life forever. The barrel racing started and one of the riders was my childhood friend and idol Fay Ann Horton Leach. The excitement was so overwhelming that I started to cry, wanting to be in that arena so badly. I fell in love with barrel racing then and there and knew that this was something I just had to do. Determined to overcome any and every obstacle, I set my sights on running those barrels just like my friend Fay.

One day, a friend of my Daddy's called and said he had a four-year-old gelding named Cebe Reed he would like me to ride. I immediately formed a strong bond with this horse; we became such a team! We broke records everywhere we

went. I knew Cebe Reed and I could be as great as we wanted to be, and we went for it. In 1967, Cebe won three horse trailers and over $12,000, which was a lot of money in those days. Because of Cebe, who took me to the barrel races and calf-roping events, I met the real love of my life, R. E. Josey.

His love for horses, along with mine, turned the next few years into Josey magic: the Josey barrel and calf-roping schools, rodeos, and world championships. Along with "Josey"—my husband and the best coach I could ever have—we have taken the family ranch and created our own world where horses are the main attraction. When visitors cross through our cattle guard, they enter a unique place where barrel racing and calf roping are common talk. When you visit Josey Ranch, you become part of the Josey team.

At home, I can look out my big kitchen window and see the barn and my horse, Orange Smash. I love this horse because he knows his job and does it well, run after run—the mark of a true champion. He and I just returned from competing at my eleventh National Finals Rodeo and look forward to what the future may bring.

The Lord has been good to Josey and me. We have been blessed with many wonderful horses over the years: Cebe Reed, with his exceptional gathering ability and unyielding desire; Sonny Bit O'Both, who had such balance and consistency; and Mr. Revolution Bars, who made running barrels fun because of his ability to run small or big patterns—he was a real turner. There have been hard times, too, but the Lord has always let us know we were doing something He approved of, as our love for horses, rodeo, and travel also involved teaching others from our experiences. I can't imagine what my life would have been like without horses in it. I can only wish that every little boy or girl be so fortunate to have a horse of his or her own.

Set your goals and don't settle for anything less. Remember, "In God, everything is possible." Follow your dreams. I did!

Martha's faith is unshakeable. Her love for kids is from the heart, and her riding abilities speak for themselves. I've had the opportunity to sit through several Martha Josey barrel clinics and the one thing that impressed me most was her ability to focus on the goal and not concern herself with the details. Sure, the mechanics of the exercises are important. I was taught, go in wide and come out tight, brace with your left and pull your rein to your pocket—that's where you put the money, *and* stay out of his mouth on the straight. *But I also learned that once you learn the mechanics, start to focus on the goal.*

We can get so wrapped up in the mechanics of the issue at hand that we forget what the issue at hand is. I've heard it said that if we were taught to walk the same way that we teach people to learn, we would still be crawling. We must remember that riding a horse, in it's basic form, is simply not falling off. Perhaps I have an unfair advantage when it comes to riding because I was not taught to ride but, rather, not to fall off. How do you learn to not fall off? By falling off, of course. Children learn to walk not by analyzing their failures but by simply getting up and doing it again until they can walk.

Sometimes it is more productive to ignore details and focus on the goal. I've often advised people who have asked me about horse difficulties that if you ignore a problem for twenty to thirty miles on the trail, it will probably go away. This is not to say that riding without thinking will solve all of your problems, but many times the details take care of themselves when you focus on the goal.

Years ago, I met B. B. King. When I asked him for some words of wisdom concerning musical performance, he bestowed upon me words that have stuck. "Learn everything you possibly can about your instrument, practice all the time and learn it good, but when you get onstage, forget it all and just play the music."

GOD'S GIFT TO WOMEN

by Lanie Frick

In riding a horse,
we borrow freedom.

—Helen Thomson

My older sisters tell me that I've been drawing since I was old enough to hold a pencil. Mama, when going to the store, would ask each of us to name one thing we would like her to bring us. I always asked for "a coloring book with no pictures in it." As I grew older, I would draw at every chance I got. I would lose myself in this creativity to such an extent that the outside world ceased to exist for me.

As I reached the age when most girls become infatuated with boys and parties, I became fascinated with horses—riding and drawing horses. I discovered the intricate beauty of horses and recognized the personal challenge they represented. Perhaps drawing horses was my way of revealing myself to others at an age when expressing oneself is so important.

Drawing is such a primal, instinctual form of self-expression. Virtually everyone draws or colors or scribbles during some stage of his or her childhood development. Through drawing, children learn what they are about and reveal to others who they are. Many a girl will draw horses even if she doesn't have one. I think this is because horses are what girls aspire to be: strong, free-willed, spirited, beautiful. This inner vision is revealed in women's drawings of horses many times over. As girls grow into young women, some begin to find self-expression through other interests. Others hold fast to their vision and see their drawing skills develop simultaneously with their personal skills. This is how it worked for me, and still does.

It is such a challenge to get a drawing of a horse anatomically correct. It is even more of a challenge to make its spirit and character come alive on a two-dimensional surface. The hardest part is learning to let go, to let your spirit and Creator guide you through the piece. This is hard because you cannot be in control of this part of the process, and human beings are extremely reluctant to relinquish control over anything, especially themselves. Only through this process of letting go, however, is the most expressive work created, and it is this expressive work that is the most rewarding.

While exploring horses through drawing, I continued my relationship with horses by riding. Eventually, I began to give lessons as my cooperative approach to riding received recognition. A dozen years or so later, I'm still giving lessons.

Most of my students seek to establish a physical connection with their horses to improve their riding. Once a rider grasps how her body works, how the horse's body works, and how the two are similar and need to work together, the door is opened for the emotional connection to take place. Often, both horse and rider experience a great release of tension. At other times, a revelation comes over the rider and the horse seems to say, *Finally! She got it!* Then the two can become one. The rider takes with her a new awareness of self and a horse she always dreamed existed.

The majority of my students are women. This holds true whether I am conducting a clinic, a private lesson, or a 4-H horsemanship group meeting. Women are so eager to learn and absorb information. They rejoice upon seeing positive results with their mounts. Women are rewarding students because most of them are willing to let go of negative habits as they grasp positive ones. They strive for true partnerships with their mounts, and a sense that rider and horse are working together in a relationship of mutual respect.

Witnessing this phenomenon take place and knowing I helped facilitate it is a joyous experience for me. I am thankful I can help others realize the unique, wonderful relationship a horse can give.

Horses are a gift. They are Creator's gift to us all. Through horses, we receive a vision of freedom, a sense of limitlessness and confident power. Unlike other animals who appear tied to the earth even in motion, horses seem to move on the breath of the wind. Perhaps this explains why horses serve as such strong inspiration to us. The word *inspiration* means "divine breath." Horses, unique among the animal kingdom, seem breathed to us directly from Creator.

There is a special phenomenon that occurs between women and horses. Women seek spiritual, uplifting experiences and horses willingly facilitate this quest. Women generally are patient, good listeners, and are eager to be heard. Horses want to communicate and are willing to listen. They appreciate a calm, gentle hand absent any agenda. Women recognize what horses offer, and horses respond to that recognition. When a girl or woman rides a horse and the bond between them is strong, she feels that nothing is impossible. She becomes the Princess, the Knight, the Warrior, the Messenger of Nature. Whatever her dreams, they become clear and attainable.

Horses give us so much: power, strength, speed, mobility, freedom, and independence. They expand our vision of what is possible, help us develop our self-confidence and facilitate the discovery of our oneness with nature. And what can we give them in return? At minimum, we can give them good care: adequate food, safe shelter, and humane treatment. Women find caring for their

horses gratifying and therapeutic, rather than a chore. To women, it is a privilege, rather than an obligation. Horses can sense this and their contentment fosters their eagerness to strengthen the bond, to share in that communion.

At the first approach, horses instinctively know what is on the mind and in the heart of the person they are facing. They can sense whether one's intent is positive or negative. They are very sensitive to everything in their environment and are observant of the slightest change in body language, vocal inflection, and attitude. Certain characteristics inspire a horse to be curious, interested, and responsive: a calm, quiet voice; soft eye contact; an easy, gentle touch; steady, even motions.

Other characteristics make a horse become fearful or aggressive: a loud, harsh voice; staring, or hard, eye contact; rough hands; quick, jerky movements. Women tend to possess the traits to which a horse responds positively. Women are naturally sensitive to the needs of others and willing to nurture positive relationships. Women are therefore willing to devote the time and attention necessary to learn the horses' language and respond to their needs. This is why the relationship between horse and woman develops so quickly and is so strong.

In the presence of horses, one recognizes something within the horse that is echoed within oneself. This creates a wonderful learning atmosphere, allowing the horse to teach us about ourselves as humans and, through our relationship with the horse, how to treat not only other living creatures but also one another. Horses are straightforward. They play no head-games. With horses, there is no deception. It is their total honesty that makes the relationship between horse and woman so rewarding.

Horses have taught me so much: patience, tolerance, acceptance, and endurance. They have taught me how to listen and how to understand and use body language to communicate. Riding horses helped me develop a sense of adventure and filled me with a desire to embrace nature. Through horses, I developed self-confidence. Above all, horses taught me the importance of respect. Respect is the cornerstone for every relationship of any kind. It is fundamental and primary in building a rewarding relationship with the horse.

It is easy to respect a horse's size and strength, for the horse is so much larger and stronger than we are. What is not so easy is to respect them as creatures having the same basic needs as humans. Horses hold their own special place on this earth. Understanding this, we then must deal with how we treat them and others of our kind. Women have a strong sense of fairness that helps them reach this necessary level of mutual respect.

I use all the lessons horses have taught me in every facet of my life. I am still learning.

Horses are patient teachers. I know this because they have taught me. I don't think that I am a particularly dense student but had horses not been patient with me, I probably would have given up in frustration long ago. My horse taught me: Pony, when you sit down, I stop; when you push me through, I continue. *Any of us can easily memorize those words in a matter of minutes, yet my horse and others have had to repeat them to me hundreds of times. My* horse did not throw me to the ground and say, *That's it! I've told you fifty times now and I'm not* going to let you on my back again. *My horse simply stopped dead every time I sat down and remind-* ed me when you sit down I stop . . . .

Lanie mentions in her essay that "Women generally are patient, good listeners, and are eager to be heard." Because women are generally patient and good listeners, their relationship with hors-es is a strong and natural one.

HORSES ARE REFLECTIONS OF WOMEN

by Barbra Schulte

God first made Man.
He thought better of it and made Woman.
When He had time, He made the Horse,
which has the courage and spirit of Man
and the beauty and grace of Woman.

—Brazilian saying

Barbra has a lovely way of talking about the rela-
tionship between women and horses. It's gentle and direct and eloquent. She
describes the relationship of the horse to women as "a kindred spirit." She says
that women "blossom" around horses.

Being accepted as a member of the herd is a wonderful thing. If you, as an out-
sider, have had the occasion to stand among a herd of twenty or more, you know the intense
intimidation that you can feel. Here you are standing among a group of powerful individuals, and
you don't know anyone. Recently, I was in this very situation and had a moment to reflect on the
emotions that ran through me. First was fear: a simple fear, which told me that at any moment I
could be trampled. Next came the feeling of being shunned. These individuals ignored me as if I did
not exist. Immediately I tried to convince these horses that I was an old pro: I've made friends with
hundreds of your species, therefore you should trust me. Still, I was shunned. Finally the feeling of

total abandonment set in. Here I was, standing among twenty-plus horses, and not one of them would so much as make eye contact with me. To make matters worse, the reason for me being among this herd was so that Gabrielle Boiselle, could get a few shots of me interacting with the herd. I was completely alone, and there was nothing I could do to make the herd accept me. This is a horrible feeling. Finally, a four-year-old buckskin stud looked my way. He only looked at me for a second or two but it was enough to say to me, We know you're here.

That little bit of acceptance was all I needed to put me at ease. Not one member of that herd was forced in any way to accept me, yet it was the horse's very nature that forced that buckskin to look my way. Acceptance is the way of the horse, and it is what so many of us crave in our day-to-day lives. These animals have no agenda. They accept us for who and what we are, and they allow some of us to blossom.

After devoting much thought to the subject of the special bond that exists between women and horses, I've come up with four realms, or reasons, for this phenomenon. First, I think that women and horses are kindred spirits. In my experience, the horse has a unique way of perceiving the world. The horse's psyche seems to be very close to my own and, I imagine, many women's. Horses are nurturing, and I believe that they are wise about relationships.

A renowned marriage and relationship counselor, Gary Smalley, said on one of his videotapes that if you ever want to know how a relationship is going between a man and woman, ask the woman. She is the one who will really understand and know. I think that in a relationship with a horse, it is the horse who really knows. If you want to know about the relationship between a horse and the rider, all you really have to do is look at the horse.

Horses represent what makes a woman a woman, the way we perceive the world, our spirit. I believe that a horse and a woman have a lot of commonalties. Those things that make them kindred spirits are nurturing, and both are wise about relationships.

Second, horses give women a specific channel by which to express ourselves—a way to let go, to live out our dreams in an uninhibited way. A horse can be soft and aggressive at the same time. I see this within my own competitive world of cutting. It's not like a lot of other equestrian sports. The cutting world is equal in numbers between men and women. There is no advantage, from a judge's point of view, if you are a man or a woman when you go to the herd. But when I see a woman cutting, her nature really adds a lot of dimension to the whole picture. I think that women somehow blossom around horses. A cutting horse, by the very nature of our sport, has to be "turned loose" during competition. The horse's intuitiveness, along with the training, is expressed when the approach is more trusting and instinctive.

Third, horses are our friends. Women love friends, lots of them, and love talking to them. One of my favorite things about being with my horses is that I talk to them constantly. I ask them how they are doing and I try to be perceptive

about how they are feeling. They are as much a friend to me as are many of my human friends. For a woman, this friendship with horses is real. I don't see the same kind of friendship between a lot of men and their horses. Many men approach their horses with the attitude, *What can the horse do for me?* For me, it's much harder when a horse won't let me in, into his heart, into his head. I have a mare who has a hard time trusting, and she can be grouchy. She'll pin her ears when a bird flies by, even when no humans are around. I care for her very much but it's more difficult with her than with other horses who are more open.

I think that horses are often reflections of ourselves, reflections of where we are emotionally and where we are in our lives. When we ride, if things aren't going well, it's usually because things aren't going very well in our own lives. I think that horses can pick up on this.

And finally, horses allow us to be our most natural selves. Most women in our culture tend to be or do whatever the role of the moment dictates, whether it be in her relationship, in her job, or with friends. But alone with her horse, because of the joy that is there, because there are no demands, there is an openness and a freedom that allows one to see more clearly what a woman is all about. Watch a woman with her horse, and you'll see that woman's real nature. For some reason, women seem to need permission to be and express who they are. The horse gives women the permission to be these things.

A GENTLY TEACHING FRIEND

by Jan Snodgrass

*There is no secret
so close as that
between a rider
and his horse.*

—Robert Smith Surtees

I am sitting on my horse Harry Who?, about to enter the cross-country start box at the 1995 Fair Hill CCI***, one of the toughest three-day events in the country. It is a sunny, late October afternoon. The air is electric. Harry is wired. Our adrenaline is flowing. We are about to jump the hardest cross-country course either of us has ever faced.

One usually likes to arrive at such a moment fully prepared in every way. That, of course, is the plan. But though we met our final qualification requirements at the end of August by going clean on cross-country and placing third at the Millbrook Horse trials, our last two horse trials had been disastrous. I fell and did not complete either one. My confidence was thoroughly shaken.

"Fifteen seconds," says the starter.

I walk Harry straight into the box, facing the back. His head is up, his body is tense, and his ears are pricked. And he has that silly look on his face that says, *Oh, boy!* He is so happy and excited he makes me laugh.

My confidence problem is nothing new. I've been battling it hard all year, this being our first year competing at advanced-level eventing. I've been battling it all my life. We had done well until I got body slammed in Georgia in September. That's one thing about eventing. If your fears don't bite the dust, you do. Of course, it's not always fear that does it. Sometimes it's just a mistake. Then you fear making mistakes.

"Ten, nine, eight . . ."

Horses have always led me to face and conquer my fears. I've had a great many fears. I remember when I was fourteen, my voice quivering as I spoke on the phone. I was afraid because I was speaking to someone I didn't know about the terrifying fact that they had a horse for sale.

". . . seven, six . . ."

I turn Harry a couple of steps to the left so he is facing the side of the start box. But the cross-country course today does not scare me, it is the way I might ride if I don't stay focused that scares me. It looked surprisingly jumpable even the first time I walked it. And, of course, my coach, Jimmy

Wofford, has assured me that if I ride exactly as he says, we can do it.

Right, Jim.

We plan to go the long way at three of the combinations. Our goal is to get around clean and safe.

". . . five, four . . ."

The hard part is controlling what is going on in my mind. A couple of weeks ago, I had trouble riding up to a jump without a momentary flash of fear. I've been able to stop that, but I have to stay focused to do it. It has been a tough few weeks, but my confidence has been restored—I think.

". . . three, two, one . . . ."

It's difficult to control an explosive horse and hit the button on your stopwatch while your hands are shaking. The shaking is from adrenaline, which I am quite familiar with because I have been running on it all week. On Monday, my barn help quit. I have four other horses; suddenly, I had a lot of extra work to do. Tuesday night, I hoped to get a good night sleep before leaving at noon on Wednesday. But I was up most of the night when my three-year-old became colicky. I arrived at Fair Hill on Wednesday evening, exhausted, with dirty tack and no groom to help me. Yes, adrenaline is a good thing.

"GO! Have a great ride."

"Thank you." I reply and we are off.

Harry loves the cross-country phase. He usually comes out of the start box like someone has shot him out of a cannon. He pulls me to the first two or three fences before he settles. But he is not doing that. I have to urge him down to the first fence. He jumps it fine. He jumps the next three okay, too, but he is not attacking, I have to push him. What's wrong?

This does not make sense and it is not good. These fences are made to be jumped at speed with a great amount of impulsion and momentum. We have gone fifteen kilometers already on the earlier phases of roads and tracks and steeplechase. Harry jumped fabulously on steeplechase, despite deep footing. He recovered very well on the second roads and tracks. I ride with an on-board heart-rate monitor, so I know exactly how he is recovering. He came into the ten-minute box in very good shape and the vets marveled at his excellent recovery. He was not just fine, he was fantastic.

The next set of fences in front of us now are two bounces up a very steep hill. We need plenty of impulsion for this. But Harry puts an extra stride in front of the first fence, loses power, ekes through the first bounce, and jumps slowly through the second. We lose time. I am puzzled and concerned. He jumps the next few fences, but speed is definitely lacking. We should be going at least 570 meters per minute. We are not. At fence nine, the Double Palisades, we go the long way as planned, making an S turn between this downhill double.

I don't know why, but I fell in love with horses the moment I discovered what they were when I was very young. Completely, helplessly in love. I thought they were beautiful. That has never changed. Since then, they have been the cause of or have influenced every major decision in my life. Horses have always been my friends. My best friends. Sometimes my only friends. They have both saved me from disaster and been the cause of disaster. I believe I actually owe my life to them.

I spur Harry to avoid disaster here. We need a lot of impulsion and a good deal of speed to get through this next uphill combination. Coming off a turn, we must jump over a very large ditch, land, then bounce over a big brush fence, take two or three strides, then jump up a bank. It's a big task that requires precision and lots of push. Harry does not like ditches, and he is not responding to my leg. I reach back and tap him with my stick. He jumps the ditch, but then stops, refusing the brush. This really surprises me. I smack him once, reorganize, and take the alternate route out. Then we canter, much too slowly, up the hill through the woods.

A couple of fences later, we're at the halfway point. I glance at my watch to find us well over a minute slow. We have a long gallop between fences here. Jimmy told me that this would be the point to really assess how Harry was feeling on course.

Harry is a funny kind of horse. Half Cleveland bay, half Thoroughbred, 17 hands of intelligence, athleticism, definite opinions, and a sense of humor. He has a distinctive style of running and jumping. He is not very fast on a good day. Right now he's just plain slow.

My concern is growing. Harry feels tired. My heart-rate monitor is giving me normal readings, though. If something were actually wrong, Harry's heart rate would be higher than normal. It is not. I'm going to have to ride him very carefully. I can't afford to make a mistake.

Four fences later, Harry struggles through the difficult Sunken Road combination. I'm not sure what to do. I consider pulling up. But you can't jump these fences thinking about pulling up. I take him down to the big log with the drop and slide. He slithers over it. At the bottom, I spur him forward. We have just a few strides to a

vertical and a drop into water. He jumps weakly over the rails. We canter through the water and up the steep little hill to the log on top. Harry stops in front of it.

I really hate to quit. We are nearly three-quarters of the way around the course. I circle around and approach the log again and again he stops. This is not normal for Harry. Something is just not right. Though we have one more chance to jump the fence, I tell the fence judge that we are retiring on course, I give Harry a good pat and tell him how wonderful he is. I'm very disappointed. It has taken Harry and me three years together to get to this point.

I've been riding for more than twenty-five years and eventing for fifteen. During that time and even before, horses have forced me to conquer fears I didn't know I had in order to fulfill dreams they created for me. They have acted as mirrors—gauges as to how I'm feeling. In all my work with them, they tell me how I am doing.

Are you patient today Jan? they ask. *Are you brave? Just how strong are you?*

It doesn't make sense for Harry to be so tired. I try him a short distance to see if he feels lame. He's fine. I begin noting his recovery on the monitor watch as I walk him back to the finish area. It's slower than normal. But he is also more tired than normal. All I can think of is that our conditioning program was wrong.

Back at the finish, people are asking what happened. I don't know, I tell them. He just didn't want to jump out of the water and that is not normal for him. He seems tired.

The vets check him and, of course, declare him fine.

Jan Snodgrass is sincere and radiant. She is always searching for a better way to understand horses. Jan writes a newsletter called The Goodpony Journal. *I believe that her success can be contributed to her sincere concern for horses. Jan interviewed me for an article in December 1998. The article was primarily concerned with my first book,* Horse, Follow Closely. *One question she asked me was, "Is it absolutely necessary to always be dominant over horses?"*

Horses are herd animals and we cannot change this. A herd is a group of individuals designed to act as one entity. In the herd, you can only be one of two things: a leader or a follower to some degree. When you are a member of a herd, you have no equals. Other individuals are either higher or lower than you in status—you cannot be on a level playing field with another member of the herd because if you were, the herd would not function as it was designed to function. Every member except the leader (the alpha) must follow another member to ensure the herd's safety and survival.

Many times I see people treating horses as equals. What most people don't understand is the amount of stress this causes for the horse. In a herd, both leader and follower have responsibilities. These natural responsibilities ensure the survival of the species. As a leader, your responsibility is to lead the herd safely with the herd's best interests in mind. If you do not fulfill these responsibilities, the herd will be following an unfit leader, and this will jeopardize the survival of the herd and ultimately the survival of the species. As a follower, your responsibility is to follow the leader, no matter what, no questions asked. If the leader takes you through unfamiliar territory, you follow. If the leader goes through a river that seems too deep to cross, you follow. If the leader leaps into an active volcano, so do you.

But there is a second responsibility of the follower that actually ensures the survival of the herd more than the actions of the leader: to continually challenge the abilities of the leader; to attempt to improve your own rank. This ensures that the most qualified leader is always in front.

If you have experienced a horse acting stubborn, what you have really experienced is a status problem in your small herd. Your horse has found it necessary to take over the position of leader because he felt he was more qualified than you were. You then ask him to do something and he doesn't, not because he doesn't want to, but because he is the leader and you do not have the status necessary to tell him what to do. You think you are the leader, your horse thinks he is the leader, and we humans label this behavioral problem as stubbornness.

Must we be dominant over our horses? Absolutely not. Horses do not understand dominance "over." They do, however, understand leadership "in front of." The reason that it is stressful for the horse not to have a strong leader is that it is much easier to be a follower than a leader. There are fewer decision to make. The challenges to your rank are less intense and less frequent. Leaders have a tough job. What is even more stressful than being a leader is to have a human herd mate who asserts him- or herself to be the leader, but does not prove this by his or her actions.

THE BEAUTY AND POTENCY OF THE BOND

by Chaia King

Through the days of love and celebration and joy,
and through the dark days of mourning—
the faithful horse has been with us always.

—Elizabeth Cotton

Many paths forged by mankind would not exist without our link throughout history with the horse. Humans have always shared this planet with myriad animal forms—all valuable and necessary to the combination of molecules called Earth—but of all the creatures, horses occupy a dynamic relationship with humans that continuously unfolds and expands. They have carried on their backs the evolving human, and as consciousness develops, so can the connection between horses and humans. The journey to discover the spiritual gifts that the horse has to offer is ongoing.

The modern world has given us amazing technologies, but I feel the need to remain attached to the living things around me. Remaining receptive to the knowledge that can be gained by interacting completely with a horse is the basic element of my personal quest for fulfillment.

The bond between women and horses may be innate and is certainly fostered by intuition and patience. Women are taught from birth to develop their nurturing abilities in the interest of the perpetuation of the species. Parenting, for women, has a relationship-centered motivation. Nonverbal and instinctual rapport with the other partner (of whatever kind) is necessary for any significant bond. This is also true of a woman's relationship with a horse. The bond takes time and requires all the skills women utilize to raise children, including patience, understanding, tenderness, firmness, and insistence.

Beyond the fulfillment of building a relationship within its own context, however, women enjoy the power of connecting with an animal of great strength and versatility. The feeling of riding represents the epitome of freedom made possible by a bond of cooperation, communication, and trust. Riding style or discipline is often secondary to the personal connection with the horse.

I have chosen dressage because harmony between horse and rider must be clear in order to execute the movements purely. Reining also interests me because it requires similar elements with a loose rein. There is a direct correlation between performance and personal interest. The way a rider thinks draws her to a particular discipline based on the approach needed to accomplish the desired result. Competition provides a visible means of measuring the relationship, yet it is not an end.

The exhilaration of running across a field can inspire horse and rider with shared adventures of no competitive purpose. Your horse becomes a friend you can trust and enjoy with no fear of agendas. Horses who have not been abused are always true to their nature and will act clearly from their instincts at all times. I have found this not to be widely true in the human world. The freedom of relating to the horse honestly and openly without fear of betrayal is a gift that opens your heart and frees your spirit. Your awareness of your intuition sharpens when you are with your horse, and your attunement to the animal expands and deepens.

Overcoming the communication barrier between a prey animal and a human (the greatest of all predators) is the first step in realizing the beauty and potency of the relationship between horse and rider. The competitive results of the bond between humans and horses can be seen by others, yet these successes are made possible by the unspoken, subtle messages that they share. The issues that can cloud human interactions with other humans are not present when working with horses.

My love for horses began in childhood. The magic and wonder I felt for the majestic equine animal is still with me today. My parents were supportive, and I think it is important that the value of a relationship with a horse be acknowledged for young girls, who seem to have a natural proclivity for horses. Books about horses can inspire them to pursue a life and close bond with horses. Walter Farley's *The Black Stallion* literary series was the hallmark of my youthful fascination with the Arabian horse in particular.

Mark and Galen Miller, owners of Arabian Nights in Orlando, Florida, have been influential in my pursuit of a life with horses. My first horse came from their farm, and the breeding pool established by Mark's mother, Bazy Tankersley—founder of Al-Marah Arabians—is the line I will use in my breeding pursuits. The genetic pool established by the family inhabits Arabian Nights. The show is a living testament that preserves the horse's role throughout history, from chariot races to liberty work. Including ten breeds in the show is a wonderful display of the variety that exists in the horse world. Horses are as individual as humans in their personalities and abilities—each breed has its gifts. The elegance and

spirit of the Arabian horse have captured my heart, and I'm now breeding my first broodmare. I look forward to discovering the relationship possible with a horse from birth to maturity.

The future holds for me projects involving the educational and spiritual applications of the relationship between humans and horses, and possibly training—thanks to the skill and knowledge of trainers who have influenced me. The value that horses and horse people have to offer the world is evolving to fit the needs of our modern culture. I feel blessed to be part of the evolution that will explore the enigmatic power of this ancient bond

Horses are prey, humans are predators. I've said it a thousand times and it still holds true, but I'm not certain it carries the amount of weight that some people have given it. Is it possible for a predator to become a member of a herd? Yes. The most obvious example, besides the human, is the dog. Given the chance, a dog in its natural, undomesticated state will hunt, kill, and eat a horse. As a matter of fact, coyotes and wolves make regular meals of mustang foals. If dogs are natural enemies of the horse, then why do my dog and horse sleep lying down, side-by-side? The answer is twofold. First, domestication of any species tames the prey or predator instinct. Domestication does not completely eliminate the instinct, as my neighbor with chickens can attest to, but tones it down a bit. Second, you do not have to be a horse to be accepted as a member of a horse family. As long as you act like a horse is supposed to act and follow the rules of the family, you can be accepted as a member of the family.

Our horses have been bred domestically for probably fifteen or more generations. We feed them twice daily, groom them, pet them, hug them, and kiss them. We have earned the trust of this prey animal. By earning this trust, we have gone around the horse's natural instinct to view us as a predator. It is important to study the nature of the horse and to realize that a horse, in its natural state, views you as a predator. This facet, however, is merely a single characteristic and does not define all that is the horse.

WHATEVER WILL BE WILL BE

by Her Royal Highness Princess Haya Bint Al Hussein of Jordan

. . . This most noble beast is the most beautiful,
the swiftest and of the highest courage
of domesticated animals.
His long mane and tail adorn and beautify him.
He is of fiery temperament, but good tempered,
obedient, docile and well-mannered.

—Pedro Garcia Conde, 1685

I have enjoyed contact with animals all my life, feeling that in some way I can communicate with them. My interest in animals ranges from mice to elephants, but the working partners who I eventually teamed myself with were horses.

I had ridden all my life in Jordan and carried on doing so during my educational years in England. During my last year of university I took a step sideways from show jumping to flat racing. I had trained for a few summers in Germany and found that being small and not so strong, I could not ride well in the German system. My demand for control of the bigger German horses meant that I always rode them slow, getting myself and them into trouble while jumping. This all came at a time in my life that was full of questions and doubts about my future, just like any other student a year away from graduation. I had majored in politics, philosophy, and economics at Oxford University. I'd had enough of the indoors during my studies and was full of doubts about entering into an office job.

I was also by this time more or less frightened of jumping after quite numerous falls. The press had covered my falls so extensively that I developed a serious phobia of anyone watching me ride. However, I was sure that the happiest moments in my life were those I was able to spend with my horses. So I started working to create a National Equestrian Federation for Jordan. I hoped that this would satisfy my own craving to be involved in the sport of show jumping, and that I could enjoy the success of young Jordanians in the show ring vicariously. During a General Assembly meeting of the Federation Equestre Internationale (FEI), I met the Irish delegate and asked if the Irish Federation would put me in touch with different trainers in order to start a training program for our young riders. They provided me with the name of Paul Darragh and Adain Storme.

I met Adain at a dinner with racing trainer Tommy Stack (he rode the famous Red Rum in the Grand National.) After discussing Federation strategy we got on to racing, and I took up Stack on an invitation to ride a racehorse. I flew to Ireland and rode his horses several times before I decided I really wanted to ride a race. And during all these risks, I had discussed with Adain my dreams, and of course my fears, to show jump. All the while, he listened and then after the early morning workouts with the racehorses every once in a while he would say that they had a show jumper or two at his and Paul's farm (in case I was bored, I could play around with it, you see).

At first, I wondered why they left me alone with their horses, but soon, I looked forward to them asking me to ride. Soon after that, I was asking them if I could ride. And not so long after that, I was asking Adain to come watch, and see if I had the right ideas.

A summer before my finals, I rode two flat races in Ireland. I decided after my no-pressure lessons with Adain that I would agree to my Federation's request to compete in the Asian Games in Hiroshima, Japan. For this, I resumed my training in Germany, and was excited to hear that Paul Darragh would also be training in Hiroshima (for the Kuwaiti Team).

I went, convinced that it would all go well.

I got through the first three rounds and made it to the finals with eleven other riders for the individual medals. Nerves caught up with me when I saw the hundreds of camera lenses, documenting my participation not as an athlete but as a royal. It is not surprising that my big mistake came at a double that was situated directly adjacent to the press stand. The fall was one of my most spectacular falls.

I was back in the hotel afterward, searching the TV channels for films to take my mind off the events of the day, I flipped from channel to channel and could only find plays and replays and even more replays of my fall. In frustration, I flipped to CNN, only to find that even they were running my fall from the most unflattering view of all. I switched the TV off and tried to look positively at my bid to fame. I would be the only member of the Royal Family to ever be on CNN with a rear view of a somersault. I decided that was it—I wasn't going in for any more embarrassments again.

I told this to Darragh. I asked him to find an amateur horse who I could eventually take to Jordan. I would do my finals and go home. Two months before the finals, he called to say that he and Adain had found a horse in Switzerland. I took a day off school and went to see it.

Happy with her, I sat in the kitchen with the family as they discussed the business. Then, Swiss show jumper Thomas Fuchs said they had never had a Princess in their yard, so it would be an honor for him if I would sit on his horse, "the best I've ever worked with."

Back we went to the school, and when I saw her I groaned out loud with admiration for her. I rode her and jumped her. Both Fuchs and Darragh must have been concerned at what must have sounded like extreme physical pain from me.

I explained to them when I got off the mare that I nearly was in physical pain because I absolutely loved her and did not want to leave the place without buying her, too.

I spent the days until my finals trying to understand why every time I tried to leave the sport, I got pulled back in by a force beyond my means to fight. Ironically, I took this incredible horse's name to be a sign that it was something that I could no longer fight. She was called Cera, from the song, "*Que Sera, Sera*" And Cera started it all.

I decided to look for a top team of horses after graduating, to compete with them, no matter what. I had always dreamed of competing in an Olympics, and with Adain Storme's and Paul Darragh's help, I put together a team of horses who could realize the dream. For three years I trained with them, and they introduced me to every detail of the sport positively. Finally, when we agreed I was ready, they gave me the gentle shove I needed to come back to mainland Europe and set up in Germany with well-known horseman Paul Shockemohle to continue my quest.

I have been here for over a year, and Team Harmony has continued to evolve and grow. More than ever, I have come to know exactly what my philosophy and approach is to the sport. I am no longer trained in the strict way that I was in Ireland but am surer of the base they provided me with, and I use it in developing my own approach from here on.

My horses number ten. Four are stallions used for breeding as well as showing. My philosophy is to look for no two the same. I enjoy their diversity and extremely different personalities. I have no two horses even remotely similar to each other, but they all jump—and how!

My approach to and philosophy for training and riding them with ambitions to be successful in top-class show jumping have three principles. First and most important I do everything in my power to make sure that they are feeling as good in themselves as they can possibly feel. The most important person in my stable is my groom Adain, who watches the horses like a hawk and knows them all personally. I have the staff scheduled so that they can spend as much time with the horses as possi-

ble. Some would say we are overstaffed. But whatever anyone thinks, the moods of each horse are followed as closely as possible. I work hard first to keep happy horses, and I know then that every one of them gives me all they can in the show ring.

The second thing is activity, which I believe is the center of a horse's life. Wild horses don't suffer from obesity, wind sucking, or many of the other conditions and habits that we frown upon. And they rarely suffer from some of the injuries that they so frequently incur as riding horses. I believe that a horse should move whenever, however it can. This makes it less bored and far less susceptible to injury. I will spend an hour on each horse a day. If I can't ride a horse due to injury, I'll long rein, longe, or even jog beside the horse on the road. They hack out for an hour in pairs. They enjoy working as pairs on the trails or the racetrack. They do not really realize that they are working when they are together.

I have a rule: no horse is made obedient in his own stall. Should any one of them need to be reminded to be respectful, it is done out of their box. The box is their sanctuary. They can feel safe there and get nothing but affection in their rooms. They always should have one totally peaceful haven.

If I do have a horse who I feel needs to be reprimanded because it has made me angry, then I know straight away that I'm angry because the horse has asked me a question I don't know the answer to. Anger is my sign that we have a communication problem that I am not able to work through. If, after asking for help, I come to the conclusion that it really is disobedience or that a horse is starting to take advantage, there is always a way around it. There must be a way without instilling fear. I am too small to ride even the smallest horse who is scared of me.

Third, I work on verbal commands and verbal communication. I aim to be able to get my horse to come, leave, slow down, and halt, move away, and understand clearly that I am pleased or displeased through my voice. I work them this way, walk with them this way, spend time in the field playing games this way. I believe they demand only consistency from us. This helps to fill their days and is separate from their grazing time or work. It is an extra part of their day, our communication time, and I spend time every night planning their days' varied exercising and comforting, so it's a mix of routine for security and variety to prevent boredom.

With all the interaction, I found one thing strange and rewarding. I live ten minutes away from the barn. Some nights, I have woken up with a very clear thought of one horse in my mind. No matter how late it is, I always check on the horse. More often than not, when I get to the stable, I have found that horse in distress for some reason. Many times, I have found, arriving before or minutes after me, one of my staff, who says, "I couldn't sleep, kept thinking of this horse." Could be cast, could have got tangled in a blanket, anything. I do not call the staff, but somehow the horses always call us.

In three years (touch wood), we've only had one colic case. It was at a show and was not serious. Since colic is often stress-related, I am proud we have had so little of it. I adore the horses, the help, and the life we all share together. Strangely, we called it Team Harmony before this all evolved, but it makes me smile. They keep me listening, hearing, and learning; they keep me living with very simple but great joy.

Competition, especially in one's younger years, can be a scary endeavor. Embarrassment is a powerful emotion. I've not encountered a more potent antidote for fear and embarrassment than horses. No matter how slow your time was, no matter how many obstacles you knocked over, and no matter how ridiculous you looked picking yourself up out of the dirt, there is always one individual who was there with you and to whom you can turn.

I can remember showing in halter when I was younger. To the spectator, halter class looks like a bunch of people standing in a straight line, holding their horses by a lead line. To the youngster doing the showing for the first couple of times, halter class looks like two thousand extremely critical adults staring straight at him and his horse. Imagine the embarrassment that I felt when the horse I was showing decided to stand next to me, perfectly square and upright, with his left front hoof planted firmly on my foot. The worst part was that after the judges and the crowd noticed what was going on, I could not get the horse to move off my foot. There I stood, 1,200 pounds resting on my instep, two thousand people laughing hysterically, and I could not move an inch. Now it is very funny, but then it was not. With a shove, I was free, and horse in hand I ran out of the arena. We went back to the horse's stall and I never showed in halter class again.

Embarrassment is a powerful emotion, yet this horse who was with me through the entire ordeal did not judge me, laugh at me, or cause me to feel embarrassed. He was there for me. That horse played a large role in my eventual decision to help people understand horses better. After all is said and done, horses have always been there for me.

THE EYES OF A LITTLE GIRL

by Patricia M. Doennig

> *The daughter who won't lift a finger in the house*
> *is the same child who cycles madly off in the pouring rain*
> *to spend all morning mucking out a stable.*
>
> —Samantha Armstrong

I think it is safe to say that the fascination most women have with horses started when they were little girls. Little girls and horses; there is an unexplainable and almost mystical connection. One thing is certain, if Santa could fulfill the wishes of every little girl in the world, there would be very few who wouldn't have a horse, or at least a pony. I was one of the lucky ones; I got my wish.

I don't remember much about my early years as they pertain to horses, but according to friends and family, my interest in them started as a toddler. My first memory of a horsey moment actually occurred on Christmas morning in 1948. I was only four years old, but I remember it as if it were yesterday. My family was spending the holidays at my grandparents' farm in Chester County, Pennsylvania, and as excited as I was about Christmas, the best part of the visit for me was the fact that my grandparents had horses.

It was still dark when my grandfather woke me and asked if I wanted to go out to the barn to help him feed the horses. He said we'd have to hurry with the barn chores and get back to the house before everyone else woke up—after all, it was Christmas morning!

It had snowed heavily during the night, so we had to make our way through sizeable drifts to reach the big stone bank barn. The horses greeted us eagerly with soft nickers, outstretched muzzles, and restless pawing. They were eager for their breakfast.

There were four riding horses kept in roomy stalls, where they could put their heads out across the mangers and nuzzle you as you walked down the aisle. I vividly remember the coziness of the barn from the horses' body heat, the wonderful smell of hay and straw, and the excitement of being among the horses.

My job was to scoop the grain into feed buckets and then carefully carry them to each stall. I was too small to pour the grain into the mangers without first climbing up on a bale of hay. I remember one by one, carefully placing a bucket of grain on a bale, scrambling up, and then lifting the bucket high enough to dump it into the manger. My grandfather, who had been busy haying and watering, called me to come and help him at the far end of the barn. I made my way to where he was busily opening the top of the double door of what was normally an empty stall. Then he opened the bottom half of the door and suggested I look inside. There stood the most beautiful pony I'd ever seen, with a big red ribbon around his neck.

Today, I know that this beautiful pony of my childhood memories was blind in one eye and more gray from old age than brown, which was his original color. His name was Pal and he was the perfect first pony for a four-year-old girl: dead quiet, totally dependable, and always patient with my attempts to ride, groom, and play with him.

I am privileged to say that Pal was one of many wonderful ponies and horses who have been a part of my life. And I can proudly say that many of the valuable life lessons I learned growing up— such as responsibility, self-confidence, discipline, and patience—came primarily from my association with horses.

What is it about the horse that is so fascinating to young girls? I don't think there is any one answer. It's a combination of factors, not the least of which is the beauty, strength, mystery, and sense of adventure that surrounds this beautiful creature.

Add all of this to the concept of sharing friendship, companionship, love, and experiences with an animal playmate, and I think you have the essence of the attraction. It is hard to imagine that any one animal can bring so much to a child's life, but the horse fulfills all of these needs and more.

It is because of my unwavering belief that the horse is such a positive influence on youth in general, and little girls in particular, that I became involved with The HorseLovers' Club for children ages eight to fourteen. I think it is imperative to develop new ways to promote the benefits of horses and equestrian sports so that our children and grandchildren will learn the same valuable life skills and enjoy the same treasured memories that we did. And most important, they will pass on the love of the horse to future generations

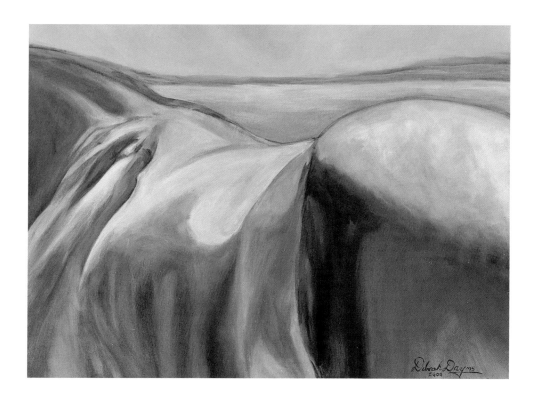

Pat Doennig is a beautiful person and a great friend.
Caring, refined, tough, down-to-earth, elegant, funny, and one of those people who gives really great hugs. If I need information about someone who participates in a discipline that I am not very familiar with, I call Pat. If I need to know something about the horse industry, I call Pat. If I want to talk with someone who will always leave me feeling good about my work, I call Pat. She has given much of herself to the horse and the people who love them.

I wish that all mothers and fathers could understand the value of a horse in a young girl's life. I'm not sure that we have enough room here in North America to get every little girl a horse or pony, but if we did, our nation would produce a generation of women and mothers such as this earth has never seen. I've met so many women, like Pat, whose lives were shaped by a childhood encounter with a horse. Whether it was a toy horse, a pony ride, riding lessons, or a horse of their own, I've seen horses help create some tremendous women.

I'm often approached by a father or grandfather asking me the "should I buy her a horse" question. My answer is always the same. "Yes, if you make only one correct decision in the raising of this child, make this be it!" I will admit to going a bit overboard on this one, but fact is I have never seen a girl for the worse because her dad or mom got her a horse. I've seen girls sail through adolescence fairly smoothly while focusing on riding. I've seen girls involved with high school rodeo avoid all of the regular traps that are encountered at their age. I've seen young women compete through their junior year in college before their interest in boys is awakened. My philosophy may be a bit simplistic or possibly even chauvinistic, but my philosophy, for the most part, works. So if you happen to be facing the question that most parents of daughters face eventually, yes would be a good answer to your daughter.

MICHELLE GRANT 1996 ©

164

THE ARTIST'S EYE

by Michelle Grant

The sight of [that pony] did something to me
I've never quite been able to explain.
He was more than tremendous strength and speed
and beauty of motion.
He set me dreaming.

—Walt Morey

$As\ an\ artist,$ I find the form of the horse is unequaled in the animal kingdom and it is most appealing to me. Horses are a sensory banquet: they look good, sound good, smell good, and feel good.

Visually, the crisp angles and planes of the face are most appealing, especially when a strong light source accentuates them. These angles and planes are repeated all over the horse's body, such as the angle of the shoulder and how it is repeated in the pastern and hooves. And the angle of the croup and how it blends so perfectly into the flowing tail. I love the legs and how they fit together so perfectly, their underlying structure just barely covered with flesh, the hocks, gaskins, pasterns, fetlocks, and hooves blending so beautifully, especially when the horse is moving. Perfection in mechanical engineering, their movement is lovely to watch and a challenge to express in art.

The surface texture of the hide I find is very pleasing to the eye, be it the glossy sheen of the athlete in prime condition, or a thick winter coat so huggable. The sun falling on these two very different types of coats, along with the numerous colors of the coat, lend themselves to endless possibilities for artwork.

The rhythmic sound of walking hooves is soothing. The pounding of galloping hooves at the track is exhilarating. The nicker of an expectant horse waiting for oats, the shrill whinny of a foal, the macho sounds of a stallion sensing a mare—it's music to the ears.

The prehensile lips and flexible nostrils, combined with a velvety texture, are wonderful indicators of character, mood, and attitude in a horse, along with a big, expressive eye. It is my goal to capture and convey these characteristics in each piece of artwork. Horses' ears are often painted in rather generic terms, and I want to push the individual onto the viewer.

I believe that women have a proficiency for seeing and appreciating the finer points of the horse. My photographer, Gabrielle, has taught me this. So have the women artists in this book. Many times, while shooting photos for Horse, Follow Closely, *I was baffled. There was Gabrielle, taking a picture of a rock or a horse's leg or a tree; and the rock to me looked like a rock. But she saw something more. After viewing the developed film it was obvious that this beautiful multifaceted stone was no ordinary rock: but it was. I was there on the day the photo was taken, and that day it was just a plain old rock. This means that when she and I looked at the same rock, we saw two entirely different images. The image that she saw could someday win some prestigious photography award, and the image that I saw was just a rock. So maybe this is how it is with horses as well.*

Yes, I have seen beautiful horses (usually the most masculine and virile looking ones), but I don't know that I have ever seen a horse like the ones women can see. Before analyzing the "rock phenomenon," I thought that maybe women were being more expressive about what they saw in the horse. Describing a horse as the most beautiful creature on the face of the earth *was, to me, another way of saying a* good-looking horse, *but I think it is more. It may be that women are seeing an entirely different image than I am seeing, and therefore describe it differently.*

I chose the artists for this book because these women were able to show me an image of the horse that I could not have seen without their gift of sharing. Perhaps I can learn to see differently and appreciate the horse even more.

167

AROUND THE WORLD
IN THIRTY-FIVE YEARS

by Julie Suhr

The rhythm of the ride carried them on and on,
and she knew that the horse was as eager as she,
as much in love with the speed and air and freedom.

—Georgess McHargue

Yesterday, I completed my twenty-five thousandth mile in endurance competition. It was a rainy November day and I spent almost eleven hours in the saddle acquiring the final miles to achieve that long-standing goal. I rode a much-loved horse. We have ninety-two years between us, so it was a golden day, despite the clouds, the rain, the cold, and the slippery trails. And at the end of the ride when my horse trotted out for the veterinarian inspection with his eyes bright and a spring in his steps, he made me a special person.

For every one of those twenty-five thousand miles in competition, there have been at least three miles in conditioning and preparation. Thirty-five years of endurance training and riding are behind me. It is a time of reflection. I have been cold, hot, hungry, and dehydrated. And worst of all, I have been scared. I am not a masochist but a hedonist because I have done what I wanted to do most.

At rides I have finished in the front, in the middle, and in the back. I have been humbled, and I have stood ten feet tall. I have greeted the dawn from the back of a horse, watched the sun set and the stars appear, and I've been guided by the moonlight. I have caressed newborns as they drew their first breath and kissed the soft muzzles of old and tired companions as they drew their last.

What possesses a forty-year-old woman to decide to sit upon a horse's back over the next thirty-five years and one hundred thousand miles? I do not know the answer. Perhaps it is hidden in the depths of a horse's eye, where untold secrets reside that we cannot probe. Or perhaps the die is cast the first time a young girl wraps her arms around a horse's neck and smells the sweetness and feels the warmth.

When I was eight, a pony awakened in me the love of the animal known as *Equus*. My pony preoccupied my thoughts as my child and my horses preoccupy them now, years later. I have never tired of feeding and caring for my horses. The happiest hour of my day is from six to seven in the morning, when I greet their soft nickers with the flakes of hay that start a new day.

It has been a privileged life. With marriage and motherhood, I thought I had left my first love behind. For twenty years, I never rode a horse or even patted one that I can remember. Yesterday, I completed my twenty-five thousandth mile in endurance competition.

When do we really know Equus? *After ten, twenty, thirty years? One hundred thousand miles? I spend almost every day of my life with the creature we have named horse, and every day I learn something from him. I have spent twenty-five years learning from and about this animal, and there are those who call him stupid. Either these folks just don't get it or I am a very slow learner. The number of people, including myself, who spend their lives teaching others about the horse, fascinates me. The horse is a complex creature with much to teach.*

A magazine reporter recently asked me, "How do you know that the horse is intelligent?" The other day, I was riding my horse Mihunka, and he stepped in a prairie dog hole and stumbled. Then he did it again and again and again. We stumbled five times in prairie dog holes and the only reason we didn't stumble a sixth time was because we ran out of holes. Had there been twenty-five prairie dog holes I am sure we would have tripped twenty-five times. I believed for a moment that I might have been on the back of a stupid animal. Perhaps all the raving I had done was simply the naïveté of a proud parent (he is my youngest). But I know better. Mihunka is the kind of horse who can practically solve multiplication problems, but he walks into closed gates. The question of intelligence in horses took some serious thought on my part.

What is intelligence? As far as I can tell, intelligence is the ability to store and process data. Most of us are very good at processing data. Give us a problem, give us the formula used to complete the problem, and most of us will do okay. Storing and recalling data is where most of us fall short of genius.

What do you think of when asked to define an intelligent person? The first thing that may come to my mind is someone with a pocket protector, but beyond that I think of someone who has a vast amount of knowledge; someone who has spent a lifetime collecting, processing, and storing data.

If intelligence depended on collecting and processing data, I would be one of the smartest humans on earth. I have in my possession most of the knowledge necessary to solve even the most difficult of problems on CD-ROM. As for processing, I don't have any problem with watching an interactive almanac on a computer screen. If only I could store all of this knowledge in my brain and be able to recall it easily, I would be considered one of the most intelligent beings on earth, aside from the horse.

I believe that the utilization of memory is the primary factor in defining intelligence. If we hold volumes of memory but cannot recall any of it, we are not considered to be intelligent. The horse has an incredible memory. I have often said that I would rather work with a wild horse, straight off the plains, than one who has had years of human influence. Most of my time is devoted not to training but to retraining. Trying to reprogram a horse proves the depths of a horse's memory. A horse who truly learns something remembers it for the rest of his life. If a horse learns that you apply twenty pounds of bit pressure to stop him, he will not stop when ten pounds is applied. If a horse is taught that leaning against the halter is okay, he will never remain tied to anything. Not until we replace his old memory with a new one will he remember things differently. And the fact that we can retrain a horse is also a testimony to his intelligence.

I believe that I am objective enough to evaluate the horse. Even though my life is filled with horses (and this may present an inherent bias) I believe I can say that the horse is intelligent and special—not just majestic or beautiful or magnificent, but special. Horses clearly have qualities that no other animals possess. They touch us in a way that no other animal can—not cows or dogs or fish or birds or cats or camels or elephants (okay, maybe elephants). Humans without horses would not be the same. Horses offer us clarity.

Afterword

"Provide me with your thoughts and opinions concerning women and horses." This was my simple request to every contributing author in this book. It turned out not to be so simple after all. Many of the women asked for clues, but I gave not one.

Never had I imagined that the significance of the equine brothers and sisters who have shaped my life could vary so much from person to person, woman to woman. This beast of burden changes shape and form depending on circumstances and the individual people whom it has encountered and to whom it is relating. God created in the horse a creature who can provide security, self-esteem, and confidence. An animal who has literally forged the lives of many, the horse has given hope, direction, and true companionship in a world in which family is being torn apart. Equus has been a cornerstone to some and a teacher of humility to others. This beast of the earth shows us power and roots. But perhaps most significant has been the horse's ability to provide fellowship. Fellowship with a member of a species who lives within its nature; who follows the rules and does not seek haughtiness or grandeur. We all know deep down that we, too, are animals, but the horse allows us to feel what it is truly like to be one.

This exploration into the world of women and horses has been an inspiring one. Although throughout the book there have been differences in opinion and even conflicts as to what the horse is, a single thread holds all the opinions together: The horse, to all concerned, embodies majesty; a dignity that cannot be found in any other creature. This understanding has given me a new image of the horse and, hopefully in turn, will provide the horse with a new image of me.

Biographies

GABRIELLE BOISELLE

Gabrielle Boiselle is a well-known international horse photographer. Born of a horse breeder family, she studied journalism and the science of communication in Munich. Gabrielle has traveled around the world photographing horses and creating breathtaking calendars and books. She is the photographer of GaWaNi Pony Boy's *Horse, Follow Closely* and *Out of the Saddle*.

FRANKIE CHESLER

Born in Miami, Florida, and now living in Ontario, Canada, Frankie Chesler has choosen to compete for Canada. She began riding at the age of four on a lead-line pony. With her Hanoverian mare, Ravenna Z, Frankie was put on the 1998-99 Canadian Show Jumping Team short-list for the first time. She was selected to represent Canada at the National Horse Show in New York, making her the youngest Canadian to ever ride on a Nations' Cup team.

DEBORAH DAY

Deborah Day grew up in a rural part of Southern California, where her enthusiasm for horses and art flourished. She graduated from California State Polytechnic University at Pomona with a major in art and a minor in animal science. Over the years she has enjoyed working with a variety of breeds in several disciplines. Deborah seeks to express her love for horses through her art.

PATRICIA M. DOENNIG

Patricia M. Doennig is a lifelong horsewoman whose career highlights include circulation manager and advertising director for *Practical Horseman* magazine; event director for the Dr. Reiner Klimke Symposiums; event coordinator for the USET's Festival of Champions; Co-Director of the World Cup Dressage Final '95; show director for the inaugural Equitana USA; managing director of The HorseLovers Club; and CEO of Equine Resources International.

LANIE FRICK

Lanie Frick is a professional artist and centered riding instructor. A lifetime of painting and riding horses has led her artwork to be published and purchased by collectors nationwide, and her riding instruction to profoundly benefit horse and rider. Lanie rides her Paso Fino horses and owns the Free Spirit Gallery in the Missouri Ozarks.

MICHELLE GRANT

Award-winning Canadian artist Michelle Grant is a graduate of the Alberta College of Art, in Calgary, Alberta. An avid horse enthusiast, Michelle particularly enjoys the nature and character of horses. She draws inspiration for her art from horse-related events that she has experienced first hand.

HEATHER E. GREAVES

As a youngster in Redding, California, Heather Greaves enjoyed trail rides and weekend shows with her AQHA mare, Sweet Bid Regaio. Heather currently manages EquiGen, an equine embryo transfer facility in Archer, Florida, with the aid of her partner, Vickie Meisenburg. Together, Heather and Vickie enjoy the company of horses on and off the job. Heather still owns and rides her old mare, Sweet Bid.

SUSAN F. GREAVES

Artist Susan F. Greaves shares her interest in horses with her daughter Heather, an equine reproductive physiologist. One of only seven artists in 1996 whose work was accepted to both the American Academy of Equine Artists Exhibition and *The Equine Image* magazine's exhibit, she won Best of Show in 1997 at the "Horses in Motion" competition at the Kentucky Derby Museum.

DR. PAMELA L. HAMILTON

Pamela Hamilton grew up on a horse farm in Michigan. She completed her undergraduate studies in psychology at Michigan State University while showing Benchmark Clarion competitively and being in Chuck Grant's Horse Capades. Her marriage to Danny Hamilton brought her to Florida, where she completed her doctoral studies in psychology. Dr. Hamilton is a frequent speaker on the relationship between horses and women, and she continues to ride and show Arabians.

LESLEY HARRISON

For over twenty-five years, this California-based pastel artist has touched the hearts of art lovers and animal lovers alike. Her portrayal of wildlife subjects and domestic animals—especially horses—are known for their lifelike realism and powerful emotion. She has published over forty-five limited edition prints, been featured in numerous books, and is a highly sought artist for shows and exhibitions throughout the United States.

HER ROYAL HIGHNESS
PRINCESS HAYA BINT AL HUSSEIN

Her Royal Highness Princess Haya Bint Al Hussein is the daughter of His Majesty the late King Hussein I of Jordan and Her Majesty the late Queen Alia Al Hussein. Princess Haya was the Jordanian National Show Jumping Champion in 1988 and was voted Athlete of the Year in Jordan in 1993. She has twice been decorated by her father for her equestrian achievements. Princess Haya represents Jordan in the World Equestrian Federation and is the Chairperson of the Middle East and Western Asia Sub-Group in this Federation.

MARTHA JOSEY

Martha Josey is the only cowgirl to qualify for the National Finals Rodeo in four consecutive decades. She is an Olympic medalist, was inducted into the Cowgirl Hall of Fame, and has the distinction of winning both the AQHA and WPRA World Championships in the same year. Chosen as the 1999 Women's Sports Foundation Female Equestrian Athlete of the year, Martha continues to compete and win on the WPRA circuit.

CHAIA KING

Chaia King is presently in dressage training with Greta Wrigly. Chaia's mare, Canadian Affair (Al-Marah Canadian Beau x TC Naari), was 1998 U.S. National Prix St. Georges Top Ten. Chaia is a graduate of American University and coauthored *Daddy Day, Daughter Day* with her father, Larry King, to help children of divorce.

LISA KISER

Lisa Kiser is the marketing manager for Equitana USA. She has also managed a Thoroughbred retraining farm and has worked in tack retailing and horse boarding. A freelance writer, she is on the editorial board of *Horse Professional* magazine and does publicity work for the Horse Industry Alliance, American Association for Horsemanship Safety, and others. She lives in Dallas, Texas.

JUDITH MALOTTE

Judith Malotte combines lifelong loves of nature, music, animals, and especially horses in her paintings. After marrying, Judith and her husband, fellow Cincinnati Art Academy student Don Ashcraft, settled in Atlanta with their son and daughter. Now widowed, Judith works in her studios at Main St. Gallery in historic Buford, Georgia, and at home with her horse, dog, and cats in the foothills of the Blue Ridge Mountains.

MARY MIDKIFF

As creator and founder of the Woman and Horses™ fitness and performance program, Mary has become recognized as a pioneer in the horse industry. She is author of *Fitness, Performance and the Female Equestrian* and is an internationally known speaker and clinician. Mary is a native of Lexington, Kentucky, and is a certified Horsemaster. She resides in Boulder, Colorado, and is an active combined training competitor.

SARAH LYNN RICHARDS

Sarah Lynn Richard's spirited and luminous paintings reflect her appreciation of the horse as a powerful symbol and friend. Drawing on her work as a psychotherapist, her studies in anatomy, and her intimate relationship with nature, Sarah explores the spirit of the horse in her art. Sarah works out of her home studio on the coast of Maine.

JANE SAVOIE

Jane Savoie was the reserve rider for the bronze-medal-winning Olympic dressage team in Barcelona. She was the dressage coach for the Canadian 3-Day Event team at the Atlanta Olympics and currently coaches several dressage and 3-Day Event riders in preparation for the Olympics in Sydney. Jane is the author of three best-selling books entitled *That Winning Feeling!*, *Cross-Train Your Horse*, and *More Cross-Training* as well as two instructional videotape series entitled "The Half Halt Demystified!" and "Riding in Your Mind's Eye."

BARBRA SCHULTE

Barbra Schulte's equestrian life includes two intertwined passions. She trains and shows young cutting horses, becoming the first woman to win several national championships. Barbra also helps recreational and competitive riders overcome fear, gain confidence, and reach their potentials through her Mentally Tough program. Barbra lives with her husband, Tom, and son, Zane.

JOELLE SMITH

Joelle Smith is a Western artist who documents living history in watercolor and oil. Her subjects are horses, cowboys, and buckaroos. She has concentrated on capturing a way of life that some thought was long gone. Joelle's work is a true reflection of her experiences on ranches throughout the West.

JAN SNODGRASS

At fourteen years old, Jan Snodgrass received her first horse, a 17-hand four-year-old off the track. So it is not surprising that she became an avid event rider. Jan has a degree in journalism and is also a TTEAM Practitioner 1. She competes in eventing and publishes a newsletter on training horses, entitled *The Goodpony Journal*.

JULIE SUHR

Julie Suhr has ridden 26,000 miles of endurance rides since she started in 1964 at the age of forty. A member of the American Endurance Ride Conference Hall of Fame, she was selected as one of the persons to represent the United States in the World Championships in 1988. Julie has completed the Tevis Cup Ride twenty-one times and has competed internationally on four continents.

DELPHI M. TOTH, PH.D.

Dr. Delphi Toth is a practicing clinical psychologist and neuropsychologist specializing in head injuries and rehabilitation as well as in animal-related therapy. She was educated at Case Western Reserve University, Harvard University, Harvard Medical School, and the University of Virginia. Dr. Toth has long been involved in equine-mediated therapeutic programs. She raises Lipizzans on her farm in northeastern Ohio.

TERRY VENTURA

Terry Ventura was born in rural Minnesota, where her love of horses and riding grew. Terry is married to Minnesota's Governor Ventura, and they have a son, Tyrel, and a daughter, Jade. Terry manages a 32-acre ranch, where she gives riding lessons and runs a breeding program through which she has raised two champion horses.

MARY WANLESS

Mary Wanless became an equestrian professional while studying for a degree in physics. She developed an effective method of teaching riding based on her understanding of the biomechanical demands of riding and the communication styles that make riding skills easy to learn. She is the author of *The Natural Rider*, *Ride with Your Mind*, and *For the Good of the Rider*.